# Credit
# CHEMISTRY

The Scottish Certificate of Education Examination Papers
are reprinted by special permission of
THE SCOTTISH QUALIFICATIONS AUTHORITY.

ISBN 0 7169 9293 0
© Robert Gibson & Sons, Glasgow, Ltd., 1999

**ROBERT GIBSON · Publisher**
17 Fitzroy Place, Glasgow, G3 7SF.

SCOTTISH
CERTIFICATE OF
EDUCATION

Time: 1 hour 30 minutes

# CHEMISTRY
# STANDARD GRADE
Credit Level

## INSTRUCTIONS TO CANDIDATES

1.  All questions should be attempted.

2.  Necessary data will be found in the Standard Grade Chemistry Data Booklet provided.

3.  The questions may be answered in any order but all answers are to be written in this answer book, and must be written clearly and legibly in ink.

4.  Rough work, if any should be necessary, as well as the fair copy, is to be written in this book.
    Rough work should be scored through when the fair copy has been written.

5.  Additional graph paper and additional space for answers and rough work will be found at the end of the book.

6.  The size of the space provided for an answer should not be taken as an indication of how much to write. It is not necessary to use all the space.

7.  Before leaving the examination room you must give this book to the invigilator. If you do not, you may lose all the marks for this paper.

## CONTENTS

In Questions 1 to 8 of this part of the paper, an answer is given by circling the appropriate letter (or letters) in the answer grid provided.

In some questions, two letters are required for full marks.

If more than the correct number of answers is given, marks will be deducted.

In some cases, the number of correct responses is NOT identified in the question.

A total of 20 marks is available in this part of the paper.

## SAMPLE QUESTION

| A $CH_4$ | B $H_2$ | C $CO_2$ |
|---|---|---|
| D $CO$ | E $C_2H_5OH$ | F $C$ |

(a) Identify the hydrocarbon(s).

| (A) | B | C |
|---|---|---|
| D | E | F |

The one correct answer to part (a) is A. This should be circled.

(b) Identify the **two** elements.

| A | (B) | C |
|---|---|---|
| D | E | (F) |

As indicated in this question, there are **two** correct answers to part (b). These are B and F. Both answers are circled.

(c) Identify the substance(s) which can burn to produce **both** carbon dioxide and water.

| (A) | B | C |
|---|---|---|
| D | (E) | F |

There are **two** correct answers to part (c). These are A and E. Both answers are circled.

If, after you have recorded your answer, you decide that you have made an error and wish to make a change, you should cancel the original answer and circle the answer you now consider to be correct. Thus, in part (a), if you want to change an answer A to an answer D, your answer sheet would look like this:

| (A̸) | B | C |
|---|---|---|
| (D) | E | F |

If you want to change back to an answer which has already been scored out, you should enter a tick (✓) in the box of the answer of your choice, thus:

| ✓(A̸) | B | C |
|---|---|---|
| (D̸) | E | F |

SCOTTISH
CERTIFICATE OF
EDUCATION
Part 1994

FRIDAY, 20 MAY
1.30 PM – 3.00 PM

CHEMISTRY
STANDARD GRADE
Credit Level

**PART 1**

| | KU | PS |
|---|---|---|

1. Atoms are made up of smaller particles. The numbers of these particles can give information about the element.

| A | The number of protons in the nucleus |
|---|---|
| B | The number of neutrons in the nucleus |
| C | The number of protons plus neutrons in the nucleus |
| D | The number of electrons outside the nucleus |
| E | The number of electrons in the outer energy level |

(a) Identify the number which is 7 for the halogens.

| A |
|---|
| B |
| C |
| D |
| E |

(b) Identify the **two** numbers which are the same in all neutral atoms.

| A |
|---|
| B |
| C |
| D |
| E |

(c) Identify the mass number of an element.

| A |
|---|
| B |
| C |
| D |
| E |

**2.** Hydrocarbons contain only atoms of carbon and hydrogen.

(a) Identify the **two** hydrocarbons which can polymerise.

| A | B | C |
|---|---|---|
| D | E | F |

(b) Identify the **two** hydrocarbons which are in the same homologous series as propane.

| A | B | C |
|---|---|---|
| D | E | F |

(c) Identify the **two** isomers.

| A | B | C |
|---|---|---|
| D | E | F |

KU | PS

**3.** There are many different types of chemical reaction.

| A precipitation | B hydrolysis | C combustion |
|---|---|---|
| D neutralisation | E condensation | F addition |

Identify each of the following types of reaction.

(a)  $H^+(aq) + OH^-(aq) \rightarrow H_2O(\ell)$

| A | B | C |
|---|---|---|
| D | E | F |

(b)  $nC_6H_{12}O_6 \rightarrow (C_6H_{10}O_5)_n + nH_2O$

| A | B | C |
|---|---|---|
| D | E | F |

(c)  $C_6H_{12}O_6 + 6O_2 \rightarrow 6CO_2 + 6H_2O$

| A | B | C |
|---|---|---|
| D | E | F |

**4.** Many compounds are ionic.

| A $(NH_4)_2SO_4$ | B $Ca_3(PO_4)_2$ | C $NH_4NO_3$ |
|---|---|---|
| D $K_2SO_4$ | E $Na_3PO_4$ | F $KNO_3$ |

In this question, you may wish to use pages 5 and 6 of the data booklet to help you.

(a) Identify the **two** compounds which consist of equal numbers of positive and negative ions.

| A | B | C |
|---|---|---|
| D | E | F |

(b) Identify the **two** compounds which, when dissolved in water, will form a precipitate with barium chloride solution.

| A | B | C |
|---|---|---|
| D | E | F |

(c) Identify the compound which could **not** be used as a fertiliser.

| A | B | C |
|---|---|---|
| D | E | F |

7

KU PS

**5.** Ion-electron equations can be used to show the gain and loss of electrons in chemical reactions.

| A $Fe(s) \rightarrow Fe^{2+}(aq) + 2e$ | B $Fe^{2+}(aq) + 2e \rightarrow Fe(s)$ |
|---|---|
| C $Fe^{2+}(aq) \rightarrow Fe^{3+}(aq) + e$ | D $Fe^{3+}(aq) + e \rightarrow Fe^{2+}(aq)$ |
| E $Cu(s) \rightarrow Cu^{2+}(aq) + 2e$ | F $Cu^{2+}(aq) + 2e \rightarrow Cu(s)$ |

(a) Identify the equation which shows iron(II) ions being oxidised.

| A | B |
|---|---|
| C | D |
| E | F |

(b) Identify the **two** equations which show the reactions which occur when an iron nail is placed in copper(II) sulphate solution.

| A | B |
|---|---|
| C | D |
| E | F |

**6.** Balanced equations can be used to calculate the volume of hydrogen produced when metals react with dilute hydrochloric acid.

$$Al(s) + 3HCl(aq) \rightarrow AlCl_3(aq) + 1\tfrac{1}{2}H_2(g)$$

$$Zn(s) + 2HCl(aq) \rightarrow ZnCl_2(aq) + H_2(g)$$

$$Li(s) + HCl(aq) \rightarrow LiCl(aq) + \tfrac{1}{2}H_2(g)$$

When one mole of zinc reacts completely with dilute hydrochloric acid, about 24 litres of hydrogen are produced.

Identify the mass(es) of metal(s) which would react with excess dilute hydrochloric acid to produce about 12 litres of hydrogen.

| A | B | C |
|---|---|---|
| 1 g of sodium | 12 g of magnesium | 32 g of copper |
| D | E | F |
| 23 g of sodium | 24 g of magnesium | 64 g of copper |

| A | B | C |
|---|---|---|
| D | E | F |

**7.** Objects made of iron are often galvanised, i.e. coated with zinc.

Identify the statement(s) which can apply to a galvanised farm gate that has been scratched.

| | | |
|---|---|---|
| A | The zinc increases the rate of corrosion of iron. | A |
| B | The zinc is oxidised. | B |
| C | The zinc attracts electrons from the iron. | C |
| D | The zinc does not corrode. | D |
| E | The zinc corrodes slower than the iron. | E |
| F | The zinc is sacrificed to protect the iron. | F |

KU PS

8. Ann added 20 cm³ of 1 mol/l sodium hydroxide solution to 20 cm³ of 1 mol/l sulphuric acid.

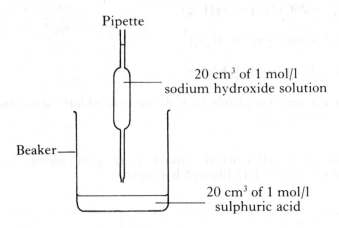

Pipette

20 cm³ of 1 mol/l
sodium hydroxide solution

Beaker

20 cm³ of 1 mol/l
sulphuric acid

Identify the statement(s) which can be applied to this experiment.

| A | The number of $H^+(aq)$ ions in the beaker decreased. | A |
|---|---|---|
| B | The pH of the solution decreased. | B |
| C | The number of $SO_4^{2-}(aq)$ ions in the beaker decreased. | C |
| D | Water molecules formed during the reaction. | D |
| E | A precipitate formed during the reaction. | E |
| F | The final solution contained equal numbers of $H^+(aq)$ and $OH^-(aq)$ ions. | F |

SCOTTISH
CERTIFICATE OF
EDUCATION
1995

MONDAY, 15 MAY
1.30 PM – 3.00 PM

CHEMISTRY
STANDARD GRADE
Credit Level

## PART 1

| KU | PS |
|----|----|

1. Many chemical compounds contain ions.

| A | B | C |
|---|---|---|
| BaO | $CaBr_2$ | CuO |
| D | E | F |
| KCl | NaBr | $SrCl_2$ |

In this question, you may wish to use the data booklet to help you.

(a) Identify the compound which gives a lilac flame colour.

| A | B | C |
|---|---|---|
| D | E | F |

(b) Identify the **two** compounds which are bases.

| A | B | C |
|---|---|---|
| D | E | F |

(c) Identify the compound in which **both** ions have the same electron arrangement as argon.

| A | B | C |
|---|---|---|
| D | E | F |

2. Hydrocarbons contain only atoms of carbon and hydrogen.

| A | B | C |
|---|---|---|
| H   H<br>$\vert$   $\vert$<br>H$-$C$-$C$-$H<br>$\vert$   $\vert$<br>H$-$C$-$C$-$H<br>$\vert$   $\vert$<br>H   H | H   H<br>$\vert$   $\vert$<br>C $=$ C<br>$\vert$   $\vert$<br>H   H | H   H   H<br>$\vert$   $\vert$   $\vert$<br>H$-$C$-$C$-$C$-$H<br>$\vert$   $\vert$   $\vert$<br>H   H   H |
| D | E | F |
| H   H   H   H<br>$\vert$   $\vert$   $\vert$   $\vert$<br>H$-$C$-$C$-$C$-$C$-$H<br>$\vert$   $\vert$   $\vert$   $\vert$<br>H   H   H   H | H<br>$\vert$<br>H$-$C$-$H<br>H   $\vert$   H<br>$\vert$   $\vert$   $\vert$<br>H$-$C $-$ C $-$ C$-$H<br>$\vert$   $\vert$   $\vert$<br>H   H   H | H   H<br>$\vert$   $\vert$<br>C $=$ C$-$C$-$H<br>$\vert$   $\vert$   $\vert$<br>H   H   H |

(a) Identify the hydrocarbon which reacts with hydrogen to form propane.

| A | B | C |
|---|---|---|
| D | E | F |

(b) Identify the hydrocarbon with the general formula $C_nH_{2n}$ which does **not** immediately decolourise bromine solution.

| A | B | C |
|---|---|---|
| D | E | F |

(c) Identify the **two** isomers.

| A | B | C |
|---|---|---|
| D | E | F |

**3.** Many chemical reactions involve water.

| A | $C_2H_5OH \rightarrow C_2H_4 + H_2O$ |
|---|---|
| B | $CH_4 + 2O_2 \rightarrow CO_2 + 2H_2O$ |
| C | $C_2H_2 + H_2O \rightarrow C_2H_4O$ |
| D | $2H_2 + O_2 \rightarrow 2H_2O$ |
| E | $C_6H_{12}O_6 \rightarrow 6C + 6H_2O$ |
| F | $HNO_3 + KOH \rightarrow KNO_3 + H_2O$ |

(*a*) Identify the neutralisation reaction.

| A |
|---|
| B |
| C |
| D |
| E |
| F |

(*b*) Dehydration is the removal of water from a compound.
Identify the **two** dehydration reactions.

| A |
|---|
| B |
| C |
| D |
| E |
| F |

KU PS

**4.** Iron(III) chloride solution reacts with potassium iodide solution in a redox reaction.

$$2FeCl_3 + 2KI \rightarrow 2FeCl_2 + I_2 + 2KCl$$

The grid shows the ions present during the reaction.

| A | | |
|---|---|---|
| | $Fe^{3+}$ | |
| B | | |
| | $Cl^-$ | |
| C | | |
| | $K^+$ | |
| D | | |
| | $I^-$ | |
| E | | |
| | $Fe^{2+}$ | |

(a) Identify the ion which is reduced.

You may wish to use page 7 in the data booklet to help you.

| A |
|---|
| B |
| C |
| D |
| E |

(b) Identify the **two** spectator ions in the reaction.

| A |
|---|
| B |
| C |
| D |
| E |

14

**5.** The grid shows pairs of reactants.

| A | B |
|---|---|
| $Mg(s) + HCl(aq)$ | $CuSO_4(aq) + Na_2CO_3(aq)$ |
| **C** | **D** |
| $Fe(s) + CuSO_4(aq)$ | $NaOH(aq) + HCl(aq)$ |
| **E** | **F** |
| $NH_4NO_3(s) + NaOH(s)$ | $MgO(s) + H_2SO_4(aq)$ |

(a) Identify the pair which will react to displace a metal.

| A | B |
|---|---|
| C | D |
| E | F |

(b) Identify the pair(s) which will react to form a gas.

| A | B |
|---|---|
| C | D |
| E | F |

**6.** The pH values of 1mol/l solutions of some salts are shown in the table.

| SALT | pH |
|------|-----|
| iron(III) sulphate | 1 |
| aluminium chloride | 3 |
| zinc sulphate | 3 |
| copper(II) nitrate | 3 |
| sodium chloride | 7 |
| potassium sulphate | 7 |
| sodium carbonate | 10 |
| potassium carbonate | 11 |

Identify the statement(s) which can be made about the salts in the table.

| A | The salts are neutral. |
|---|------------------------|
| B | The salts of transition metals are acidic. |
| C | The sulphates are acidic. |
| D | The salts of group I metals are neutral. |
| E | The salts of hydrochloric acid are neutral. |

| |
|---|
| A |
| B |
| C |
| D |
| E |

**7.** 2 mol/l hydrochloric acid is often used in the chemistry laboratory.

Identify the correct statement(s) about this solution.

| A | It produces hydrogen when electrolysed. |
|---|---|
| B | It contains more $H^+(aq)$ ions than $Cl^-(aq)$ ions. |
| C | It does not react with magnesium. |
| D | $20\,cm^3$ is neutralised by $40\,cm^3$ of 1 mol/l sodium hydroxide. |
| E | $200\,cm^3$ contains one mole of hydrogen chloride. |

| |
|---|
| A |
| B |
| C |
| D |
| E |

8. Electricity is passed through copper(II) dichromate solution.

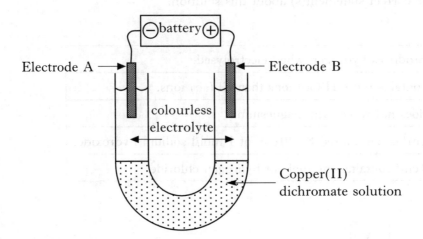

Copper(II) dichromate solution contains blue copper ions and orange dichromate ions.

Identify the correct statement(s).

| A | Copper forms at electrode A. |
|---|---|
| B | The electrolyte around electrode A remains colourless. |
| C | A blue colour moves to electrode B. |
| D | Dichromate ions move to electrode B. |
| E | Electrons move through the solution from A to B. |

| A |
|---|
| B |
| C |
| D |
| E |

9. The table shows information about some common substances which are gases at room temperature.

| Substance | Relative formula mass | Density of gas relative to hydrogen | Boiling point /°C |
|---|---|---|---|
| methane | 16 | 7 | −182 |
| neon | 20 | 9 | −249 |
| carbon monoxide | 28 | 12 | −199 |
| oxygen | 32 | 14 | −218 |
| argon | 40 | 18 | −189 |

Identify the statement(s) which the information supports.

| A | Compounds have greater densities than elements. |
|---|---|
| B | The density of a gas increases with the increase in relative formula mass. |
| C | Gases which are diatomic elements have greater densities than monatomic elements. |
| D | The boiling point of a substance does **not** depend on the relative formula mass. |

| A |
|---|
| B |
| C |
| D |

**PART 2**

*Marks*  KU  PS

**A total of 40 marks is available in this part of the paper.**

**10.** There are two different types of lithium atom $^6_3$Li and $^7_3$Li. Lithium has a relative atomic mass of 6·9.

(a) What name is used to describe the different types of lithium atom?

_____ **1**

(b) What can be said about the proportions of each type of atom in lithium?

_____

_____

_____ **1**

(c) Complete the table to show the numbers of protons, neutrons and electrons in the $^7_3$Li$^+$ ion.

| PARTICLE | NUMBER |
|---|---|
| protons | |
| neutrons | |
| electrons | |

**2**

**(4)**

*Marks*

| | KU | PS |

**11.** Solders are alloys of lead (melting point 327 °C) and tin (melting point 232 °C).

The table shows the melting points of solders containing different percentages of tin.

| Percentage tin in solder (by mass) | Melting point /°C |
|---|---|
| 10 | 305 |
| 20 | 280 |
| 30 | 260 |
| 40 | 240 |
| 50 | 215 |
| 60 | 190 |
| 70 | 190 |
| 80 | 200 |
| 90 | 215 |

(*a*) Draw a line graph of melting point against the percentage tin in solders.

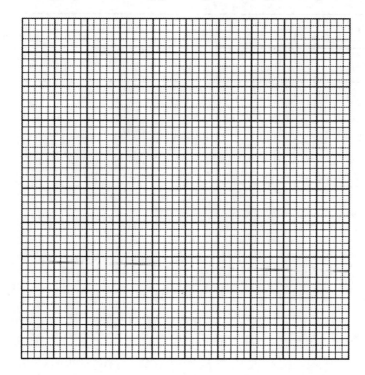

2

(*b*) State the percentage of lead present in the solder with the lowest melting point.

_____

1

Marks | KU | PS

(c) Why are alloys of metals made?

_____

_____

_____

_____

1

(d) Solders which do not contain lead are made. They are used to solder pipes for drinking water.

Suggest why this has been done.

_____

_____

_____

_____

1

(5)

Marks | KU | PS

**12.** Water in swimming pools can be purified using a chlorinating cell. Sodium chloride solution is electrolysed in the cell to produce chlorine.

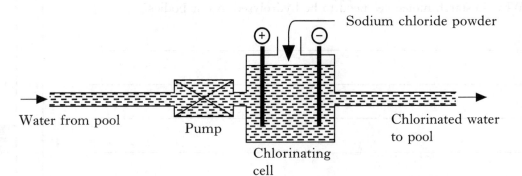

Sodium chloride powder

Water from pool

Pump

Chlorinating cell

Chlorinated water to pool

(*a*) (i) What is meant by electrolysis?

_____

_____ 1

(ii) Why can solid sodium chloride not be electrolysed?

_____

_____ 1

(*b*) Write the ion electron equation showing the formation of chlorine.

_____ 1

(*c*) Chlorine reacts with water.

$$Cl_2(g) + H_2O(\ell) \rightarrow 2H^+(aq) + OCl^-(aq) + Cl^-(aq)$$

What happens to the pH of the water in the swimming pool when it is chlorinated?

_____

_____

_____ 1

(4)

**13.** Many of the foods we eat contain starch. The starch molecules are hydrolysed in our bodies.

*Marks*  KU  PS

(a) Why do starch molecules need to be hydrolysed in our bodies?

_____

_____

_____

_____    1

(b) Why do foods containing glucose give us energy faster than starch foods?

_____

_____

_____

_____    1

(2)

| Marks | KU | PS |
|---|---|---|

**14.** Zinc reacts with sulphuric acid to produce hydrogen.

Adding copper sulphate solution is thought to speed up the reaction.

You are given the following chemicals.

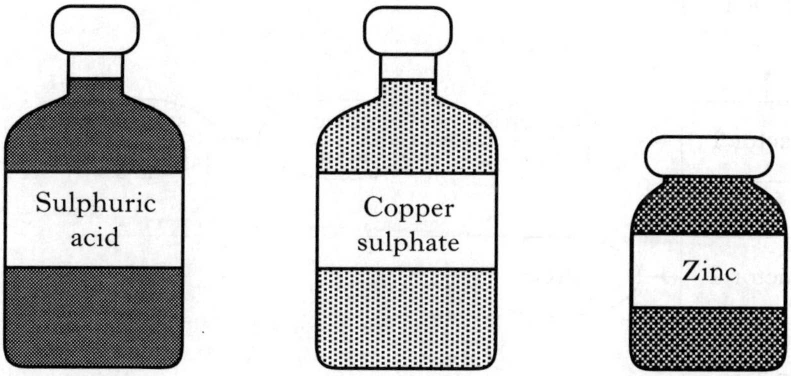


1 mol/l sulphuric acid

1 mol/l copper sulphate

Zinc lumps

Describe how you would investigate the effect of adding copper sulphate solution on the speed of the reaction between zinc and sulphuric acid.

_______________________________________________

_______________________________________________

_______________________________________________

_______________________________________________

_______________________________________________

_______________________________________________

_______________________________________________ **(2)**

Marks | KU | PS

**15.** Ammonia is an important starting material for the manufacture of other chemicals.

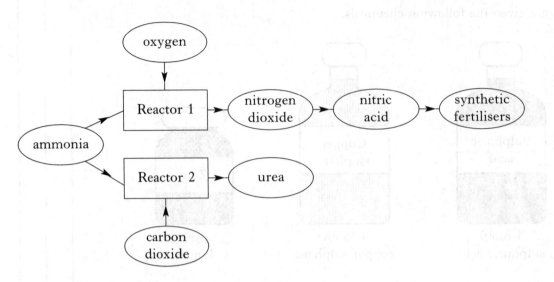

*(a)* Why is it necessary to manufacture synthetic fertilisers?

_____

_____

_____

_____    1

*(b)* Why is nitrogen dioxide made from ammonia and not from nitrogen?

_____

_____

_____    1

1995

*Marks* KU PS

(c) The reaction in Reactor 1 is exothermic.
Why is this an advantage?

_____

_____

_____

_____ **1**

(d) Urea has the following structural formula.

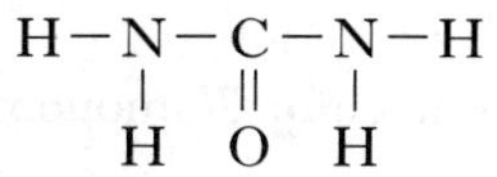

$$H-N-C-N-H$$
$$\ \ \ \ |\ \ \ \ ||\ \ \ \ |$$
$$\ \ \ \ H\ \ \ O\ \ \ H$$

Calculate the percentage by mass of nitrogen in urea.
**Show your working clearly.**

**2**

(e) Urea can also be used to make a thermosetting polymer.
What is meant by a **thermosetting** polymer?

_____

_____

_____

_____ **1**

**(6)**

27

Marks | KU | PS

**16.** Polyvinylidene chloride is an addition polymer. It is added to carpet fabrics to reduce flammability. It is made from the monomer vinylidene chloride. Part of the polymer chain is shown below.

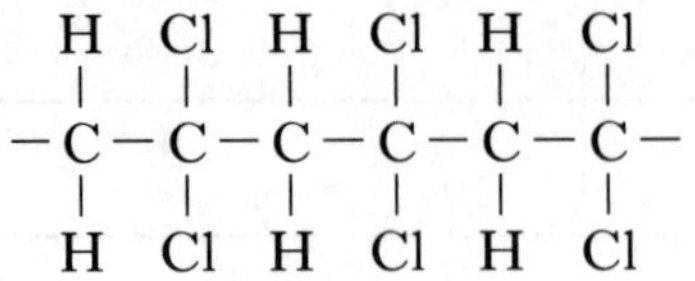

$$
\begin{array}{cccccc}
\text{H} & \text{Cl} & \text{H} & \text{Cl} & \text{H} & \text{Cl} \\
| & | & | & | & | & | \\
-\text{C}- & \text{C}- & \text{C}- & \text{C}- & \text{C}- & \text{C}- \\
| & | & | & | & | & | \\
\text{H} & \text{Cl} & \text{H} & \text{Cl} & \text{H} & \text{Cl}
\end{array}
$$

(a) What is meant by an **addition** polymer?

_____

_____  1

(b) Draw the full structural formula of the vinylidene chloride monomer.

1

(c) State a problem associated with the burning of polymers.

_____

_____  1

(d) Many polymers are **not** biodegradable.
   Why might this be an advantage?

_____

_____

_____  1

(4)

28

**17.** Toners for colouring black and white photographs are made by mixing two solutions. The solutions should be made up using warm water.

| Solution 1 |
|---|
| Sodium sulphide solution concentration 100g/l |

| Solution 2 |
|---|
| Sodium hydroxide solution concentration 80g/l |

(a) Why is **warm** water used to make up the solutions?

_____

_____

_____

1

(b) Calculate the concentration of sodium hydroxide in mol/l.
**Show your working clearly.**

2

(c) Different colours are obtained by mixing the two solutions.

| | Toner Composition | |
|---|---|---|
| Colour | Volume of sodium sulphide solution/cm$^3$ | Volume of sodium hydroxide solution/cm$^3$ |
| cold brown | 10 | 40 |
| brown | 20 | 30 |
| warm brown | 30 | 20 |

What mass of sodium sulphide will be required to make 100 cm$^3$ of toner for a cold brown colour?
**Show your working clearly.**

2

**(5)**

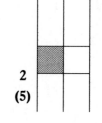

Marks KU PS

**18.** Alkanes can be made by the reaction of sodium with iodoalkanes. This is called the Wurtz synthesis.

For example, ethane can be made from iodomethane.

$$\begin{array}{c} H \\ | \\ H-C-I \\ | \\ H \end{array} + 2Na + \begin{array}{c} H \\ | \\ I-C-H \\ | \\ H \end{array} \rightarrow \begin{array}{c} H\ \ H \\ |\ \ \ | \\ H-C-C-H \\ |\ \ \ | \\ H\ \ H \end{array} + 2NaI$$

iodomethane　　　　　iodomethane

(a) Name the alkane which forms when sodium reacts with iodoethane.

_____   1

(b) Two different iodoalkanes are used to make propane.
Name the two iodoalkanes.

_____

_____   1

(c) The Wurtz synthesis can also be used to make cycloalkanes.
Draw the full structural formula of the compound which could be used to make cyclobutane.

1

(3)

**19.** "Superpure" germanium is used in transistors. There are three steps in the process used to purify germanium.

> Step 1.  $Ge(s) + 2Cl_2(g) \rightarrow GeCl_4 (\ell)$
>
> Step 2.  Water is added to the germanium chloride to form germanium dioxide and hydrogen chloride
>
> Step 3.  $GeO_2(s) + 2H_2(g) \rightarrow Ge(s) + 2H_2O(g)$

(a) Germanium chloride melts at $-49\,°C$ and boils at $84\,°C$.

State the type of bonding in germanium chloride.

_____  1

(b) (i) Balance the equation for the reaction taking place in Step 2.

$$H_2O \quad + \quad GeCl_4 \quad \rightarrow \quad GeO_2 \quad + \quad HCl$$  1

(ii) Why could the hydrogen chloride be an important product in the process?

_____

_____

_____  1

(c) What name is given to the type of reaction in Step 3?

_____  1

(d) Germanium is so similar to silicon that it was once called "eka silicon". Why are germanium and silicon similar to each other?

_____

_____

_____  1

**(5)**

*[END OF QUESTION PAPER]*

SCOTTISH
CERTIFICATE OF
EDUCATION
1996

WEDNESDAY, 15 MAY
1.30 PM – 3.00 PM

CHEMISTRY
STANDARD GRADE
Credit Level

# PART 1

|  |  |
|---|---|
| KU | PS |

1. Many of the elements in the Periodic Table are metals.

| A | B | C |
|---|---|---|
| aluminium | calcium | iron |
| D | E | F |
| lead | platinum | potassium |

   (a) Identify the metal which is used as a catalyst in the manufacture of ammonia.

   | A | B | C |
   |---|---|---|
   | D | E | F |

   (b) Identify the **two** transition metals.

   | A | B | C |
   |---|---|---|
   | D | E | F |

   (c) Identify the metal which has the lowest density.
       You may wish to refer to page 2 of your data booklet.

   | A | B | C |
   |---|---|---|
   | D | E | F |

**2.** Distillation of crude oil produces several fractions.

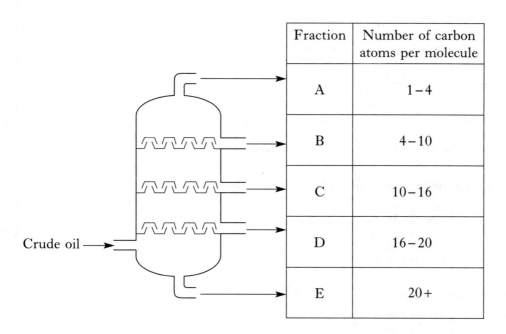

| Fraction | Number of carbon atoms per molecule |
|----------|-------------------------------------|
| A | 1–4 |
| B | 4–10 |
| C | 10–16 |
| D | 16–20 |
| E | 20+ |

Crude oil →

(a) Identify the fraction which is used as a fuel for jet aircraft.

| A |
|---|
| B |
| C |
| D |
| E |

(b) Identify the fraction with the lowest boiling point.

| A |
|---|
| B |
| C |
| D |
| E |

3. Many compounds contain carbon, hydrogen and oxygen.

| A | B | C |
|---|---|---|
| ethanol | fructose | glucose |
| D | E | F |
| maltose | starch | sucrose |

(a) Identify the **two** compounds with molecular formula $C_{12}H_{22}O_{11}$.

| A | B | C |
|---|---|---|
| D | E | F |

(b) Identify the polymer.

| A | B | C |
|---|---|---|
| D | E | F |

4. Many compounds are formed from two elements.

| A | B | C |
|---|---|---|
| $CuBr_2$ | $Fe_2O_3$ | $K_2O$ |
| D | E | F |
| LiCl | $NO_2$ | $SiO_2$ |

(a) Identify the **two** compounds which are covalent.

| A | B | C |
|---|---|---|
| D | E | F |

(b) Identify the compound which dissolves in water to give an alkaline solution.

| A | B | C |
|---|---|---|
| D | E | F |

34

**5.** Magnesium sulphate can be converted to magnesium nitrate in two stages as follows.

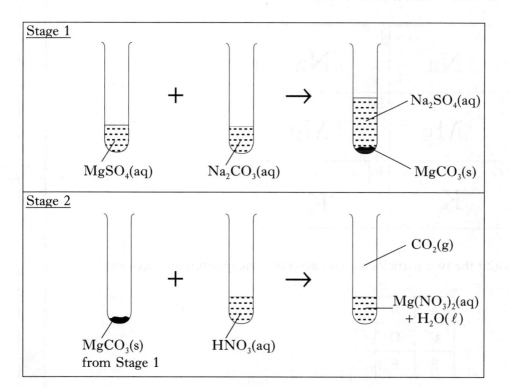

| A | B | C |
|---|---|---|
| reduction | oxidation | neutralisation |
| D | E | F |
| precipitation | addition | displacement |

(a) Identify the type of reaction involved in Stage 1.

| A | B | C |
|---|---|---|
| D | E | F |

(b) Identify the type of reaction involved in Stage 2.

| A | B | C |
|---|---|---|
| D | E | F |

KU PS

6.  Nuclide notation is used to identify atoms and ions.

| A $^{24}_{11}Na$ | B $^{23}_{11}Na^+$ |
| C $^{24}_{12}Mg$ | D $^{24}_{12}Mg^{2+}$ |
| E $^{39}_{19}K$ | F $^{40}_{19}K^+$ |

(a) Identify the **two** particles which have the same electron arrangement.

| A | B |
|---|---|
| C | D |
| E | F |

(b) Identify the **two** particles which have the same number of protons and also the same number of neutrons.

| A | B |
|---|---|
| C | D |
| E | F |

**7.** The grid gives information about the melting points and boiling points of some compounds.

| Compound | Melting point/°C | Boiling point/°C |
|---|---|---|
| A | 7 | 81 |
| B | 80 | 218 |
| C | −160 | −14 |
| D | −79 | 138 |
| E | 41 | 182 |
| F | −124 | 21 |

Identify the **two** compounds which are liquids at room temperature (25 °C).

| |
|---|
| A |
| B |
| C |
| D |
| E |
| F |

KU PS

**8.** Sulphur compounds are added to natural gas to give it a smell.

| | |
|---|---|
| **A**<br><br>$CH_3 - S - CH_3$ | **B**<br><br>$CH_3 - S - C_2H_5$ |
| **C**<br><br>$C_2H_5 - S - C_2H_5$ | **D**<br><br>$CH_3 - \overset{\displaystyle CH_3}{\underset{\displaystyle H}{\overset{\displaystyle \vert}{\underset{\displaystyle \vert}{C}}}} - S - H$ |
| **E**<br><br>$C_2H_5 - \overset{\displaystyle CH_3}{\underset{\displaystyle CH_3}{\overset{\displaystyle \vert}{\underset{\displaystyle \vert}{C}}}} - S - H$ | **F**<br><br>$\begin{matrix} CH_2 - CH_2 \\ \vert \quad\quad \vert \\ CH_2 \quad CH_2 \\ \searrow S \swarrow \end{matrix}$ |

(a) Identify the compound belonging to a series with the general formula $C_nH_{2n}S$.

| | |
|---|---|
| A | B |
| C | D |
| E | F |

(b) Identify the **two** isomers.

| | |
|---|---|
| A | B |
| C | D |
| E | F |

**9.** The voltages between pairs of metals can be used to place them in an electrochemical series.

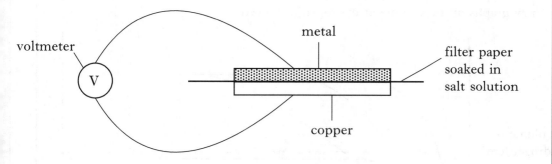

| Metal | Voltage | Direction of electron flow |
|-------|---------|-----------------------------|
| 1 | 0·6 | metal ⟶ copper |
| 2 | 0·2 | copper ⟶ metal |
| 3 | 0·9 | metal ⟶ copper |
| 4 | 0·1 | copper ⟶ metal |

Identify the correct statement(s).

| | |
|---|---|
| A | Metal 1 is the least reactive metal. |
| B | Metal 3 is found uncombined in the Earth's crust. |
| C | Metals 2 and 4 are the easiest to obtain from their compounds. |
| D | Metal 3 displaces the other metals from solutions of their salts. |
| E | Metals 1 and 3 give a higher voltage than any other pair when connected in a cell. |

| |
|---|
| A |
| B |
| C |
| D |
| E |

KU PS

**10.** Rachel investigated the reaction of zinc and hydrochloric acid. She carried out four experiments.

In each case, all the zinc reacted.

She drew graphs of the volume of hydrogen produced.

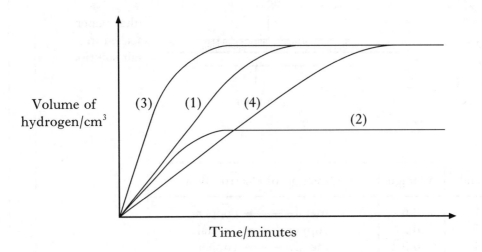

Graph 1 was obtained using 1 g zinc powder and 1 mol/l acid at 20 °C.

Identify the correct statement(s).

| | |
|---|---|
| A | Graph 2 could have been obtained using 1 g zinc powder and 1 mol/l acid at 10 °C. |
| B | Graph 2 could have been obtained using 0·5 g zinc powder and 1 mol/l acid at 20 °C. |
| C | Graph 3 could have been obtained using 1 g zinc powder and 0·5 mol/l acid at 20 °C. |
| D | Graph 4 could have been obtained using 1 g zinc powder and 1 mol/l acid at 30 °C. |
| E | Graph 4 could have been obtained using 1 g zinc lumps and 1 mol/l acid at 20 °C. |

| |
|---|
| A |
| B |
| C |
| D |
| E |

KU  PS

**PART 2**

**A total of 40 marks is available in this part of the paper.**

Marks

KU | PS

11.  Tetrafluoromethane is a covalent compound.
     Its formula is $CF_4$.

(a) Draw a diagram to show the **shape** of a molecule of tetrafluoromethane.

1

(b) The atoms in a hydrogen molecule are held together by a covalent bond.

A covalent bond is a shared pair of electrons.

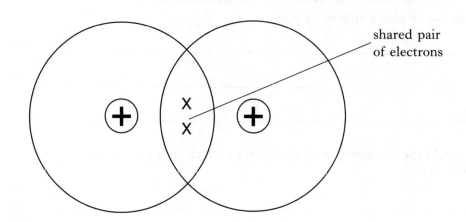

shared pair
of electrons

Explain how this holds the atoms together.

_____

_____

_____

_____

1

(2)

**12.** Alums are a group of ionic compounds. Some of them are shown in the table.

| Common name | Chemical name | Formula |
|---|---|---|
| ammonium alum | aluminium ammonium sulphate | $NH_4Al(SO_4)_2$ |
| chrome alum | chromium(III) potassium sulphate | $KCr(SO_4)_2$ |
| potash alum | | $KAl(SO_4)_2$ |
| ferric alum | ammonium iron(III) sulphate | |

Complete the table by writing in

(a) the chemical name for potash alum

(b) the formula for ferric alum.

**(2)**

**13.** Some plants can convert atmospheric nitrogen into nitrogen compounds. This is called fixing nitrogen.

Scientists are trying to develop cereal crops which fix nitrogen.

(a) How are some plants able to fix nitrogen?

_____

_____

_____    1

(b) Why would the development of cereal crops which fix nitrogen save on energy costs?

_____

_____

_____    1

(c) Name the **industrial** process which is used to fix nitrogen.

_____    1

**(3)**

*Marks* | KU | PS

**14.** When methane is passed over a platinum catalyst, other alkanes and a cycloalkane are produced.

methane → $C_2H_6$, $C_3H_8$, $C_4H_{10}$, $C_5H_{12}$ + 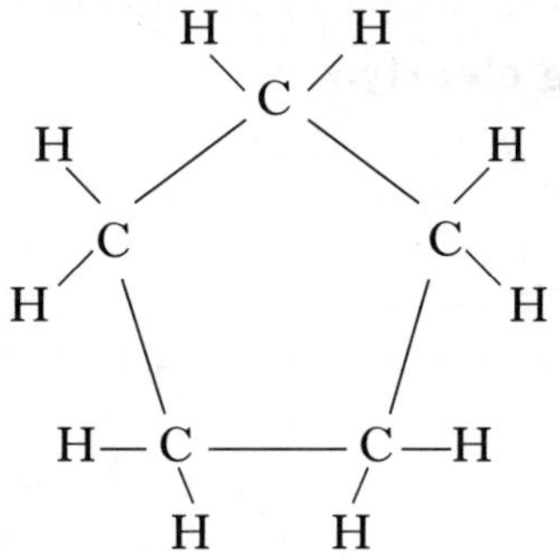

alkanes

cycloalkane

(*a*) State the general formula of the alkanes.

________________________________________ **1**

(*b*) Name the cycloalkane produced in the above reaction.

________________________________________ **1**

(*c*) Draw the full structural formula of an isomer of this cycloalkane.

**1**

**(3)**

Marks KU PS

**15.** A compound of sulphur and phosphorus is used to make matchheads.

A sample weighing 11 g is found to contain 4·8 g sulphur.

Work out the empirical (simplest) formula of the compound.

**Show your working clearly.**

(2)

**16.** Archaeologists found some corroded silver coins and a badly rusted sword.

(a) The silver coins were restored by wrapping them in zinc foil in a beaker of salt solution.

What type of reaction took place?

_____ 1

(b) The iron blade of the sword was attached to its handle by a copper band. Explain why, although the copper was uncorroded, the iron had rusted badly.

_____

_____

_____

_____ 2

(3)

1996

**17.** Mr Young gave his class three bottles labelled A, B and C.

They contained silver nitrate solution, dilute hydrochloric acid and glucose solution.

He asked the class to use the following apparatus to identify the solutions.

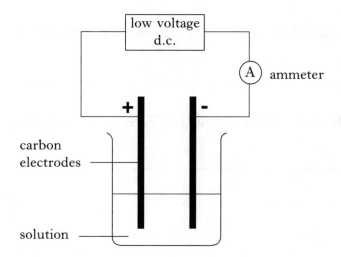

Here are the results for one group of pupils.

| Solution | Meter reading | Observations at electrodes |
|---|---|---|
| A | No | no reaction |
| B | Yes | grey solid formed at negative electrode |
| C | Yes | a gas formed at both electrodes |

(a) (i) Identify solution A.

_____  1

(ii) What type of bonding must A have?

_____  1

*Marks*

KU  PS

45

*Marks* | KU | PS

(b)  Identify solution B.

_____  **1**

(c)  (i)  Name the gas formed at the negative electrode when solution C is used.

_____  **1**

(ii)  Describe another test which could be used to confirm the identity of solution C.

_____

_____  **1**

**(5)**

**18.** Methane can be prepared in the laboratory.

To burn the gas, it is bubbled through water to monitor the flow rate, then passed through lumps of calcium chloride to dry it.

Complete and label the diagram to show the arrangement you would use to do this.

*Marks* | KU | PS

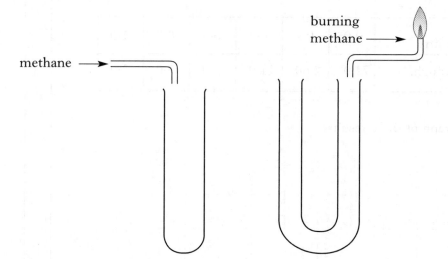

(2)

**19.** Copper(II) sulphate solution is blue. When it is placed in a beam of light, some of the light is absorbed and some passes through.

David investigated this effect to see if the amount of light passing through depends on the concentration of the copper(II) sulphate solution.

He obtained the following results:

| Concentration of $CuSO_4$/moles per litre | 0·05 | 0·2 | 0·4 | 0·6 | 0·8 | 1·0 |
|---|---|---|---|---|---|---|
| Light passing through/% | 74·0 | 29·0 | 11·0 | 5·0 | 3·0 | 2·0 |

(a) Draw a line graph of these results.

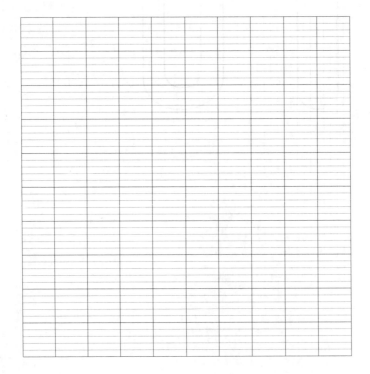

2

(b) State the relationship between the amount of light passing through and the concentration of the copper(II) sulphate solution.

1

(c) Use your graph to estimate the concentration of a copper(II) sulphate solution which allows 50% of the light to pass through.

1

**(4)**

Marks

| KU | PS |
| --- | --- |

**20.** The diagram shows how sulphur dioxide is removed from the gases given off in a coal-fired power station.

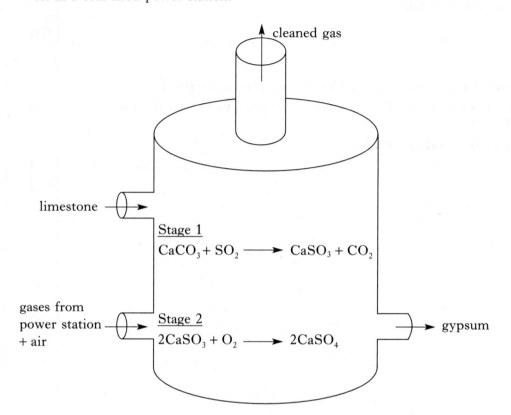

The gases given off are passed through powdered limestone (calcium carbonate) in water.

(a) Why should sulphur dioxide be removed?

_____

_____

_____   1

(b) Limestone is insoluble in water. A soluble carbonate would be more efficient. Suggest why limestone is used.

_____

_____

_____   1

*Marks* | KU | PS

(c) Give the chemical name for gypsum.

_____

1

(d) A power station produces 580 tonnes of sulphur dioxide per day.

Calculate the mass of calcium carbonate required to remove this completely.

**Show your working clearly.**

2

(5)

**21.** (*a*) Calculate the mass of sodium hydroxide which would be required to make 1 litre of exactly 1 mol/l solution.

**Show your working clearly.**

Marks

1

(*b*) Solid sodium hydroxide often contains sodium carbonate as an impurity. This is caused by some of the sodium hydroxide reacting with carbon dioxide from the air.

---

INSTRUCTION CARD

Preparation of approximately 1 mol/l sodium hydroxide solution

<u>CARE</u>: Sodium hydroxide is highly corrosive.

1. Weigh out 41 g of sodium hydroxide pellets.
2. Dissolve in about 400 cm³ of water.
3. Add a few drops of barium chloride solution to remove the carbonate ions.
4. Filter.
5. Make the volume of solution up to exactly 1 litre.

---

*Marks* KU PS

The equation for Step 3 is:

$$BaCl_2(aq) + Na_2CO_3(aq) \longrightarrow BaCO_3(s) + 2NaCl(aq)$$

(i) Name an ion which will be an impurity in the final sodium hydroxide solution.

_____   1

(ii) Rewrite the equation as an ionic equation omitting spectator ions.

_____   1

(iii) $25 \cdot 0\,cm^3$ of the solution was neutralised by $25 \cdot 5\,cm^3$ of $1\,mol/l$ hydrochloric acid.

Calculate the exact concentration of the sodium hydroxide solution.

**Show your working clearly.**

2

(5)

**22.** Sodium sulphite solution reacts with bromine solution. The sulphite ions are oxidised. The ion-electron equation for the oxidation reaction is:

$$SO_3^{2-}(aq) + H_2O(\ell) \longrightarrow SO_4^{2-}(aq) + 2H^+(aq) + 2e$$

This reaction takes place in the cell shown.

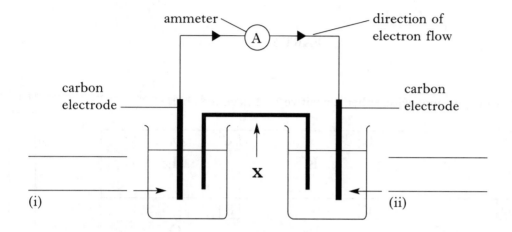

(a) On the diagram, label the two solutions at (i) and (ii) so that the flow of electrons is in the direction shown.

1

(b) What is the purpose of the filter paper (**X**) soaked in electrolyte between the beakers?

1

(c) In the reaction, the bromine solution is reduced.
Write the ion-electron equation for this reaction.

1

(d) If samples of the two solutions were mixed, what would you see happening?

1

**(4)**

*[END OF QUESTION PAPER]*

SCOTTISH
CERTIFICATE OF
EDUCATION
1997

MONDAY, 19 MAY
1.00 PM – 2.30 PM

CHEMISTRY
STANDARD GRADE
Credit Level

## PART 1

1.  Atoms can form ions with either a positive or a negative charge.

KU | PS

| A $Li^+$ | B $K^+$ | C $Mg^{2+}$ |
|---|---|---|
| D $Cl^-$ | E $Br^-$ | F $O^{2-}$ |

(a)  Identify the **two** ions with the same electron arrangement as an argon atom.
(You may wish to refer to page 1 of your data booklet.)

| A | B | C |
|---|---|---|
| D | E | F |

(b)  Identify the **two** ions which combine to form an insoluble substance.
(You may wish to refer to page 5 of your data booklet.)

| A | B | C |
|---|---|---|
| D | E | F |

2. When sodium chloride solution is electrolysed, hydrogen gas is given off at the negative electrode.

A pupil wanted to investigate if the voltage used in the process affects the rate at which hydrogen is given off.

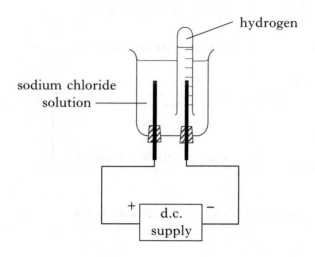

Identify the **two** experiments he should carry out to make a fair comparison.

|   | Concentration of solution (mol/l) | Type of electrode | Voltage (V) |
|---|---|---|---|
| A | 1·0 | carbon | 2·0 |
| B | 2·0 | platinum | 4·0 |
| C | 2·0 | carbon | 2·0 |
| D | 2·0 | platinum | 2·0 |
| E | 1·0 | platinum | 4·0 |
| F | 4·0 | carbon | 4·0 |

| A |
|---|
| B |
| C |
| D |
| E |
| F |

**3.** Many pairs of chemicals react together.

| | |
|---|---|
| **A**<br>ammonium chloride<br>+<br>sodium hydroxide solution | **B**<br>silver<br>+<br>dilute hydrochloric acid |
| **C**<br>copper oxide<br>+<br>dilute sulphuric acid | **D**<br>sodium hydroxide solution<br>+<br>dilute nitric acid |
| **E**<br>sodium<br>+<br>water | **F**<br>zinc<br>+<br>copper sulphate solution |

(*a*) Identify the pair(s) of chemicals which react to produce a gas.

| | |
|---|---|
| A | B |
| C | D |
| E | F |

(*b*) Identify the pair of chemicals which will **not** react.

| | |
|---|---|
| A | B |
| C | D |
| E | F |

1997

**4.** The grid shows the formulae for a number of hydrocarbons.

| A | B |
|---|---|
| $CH_3-CH-CH_3$ with $CH_3$ below | $CH_2$ over $CH_2-CH_2$ |
| C | D |
| $CH_2-CH_2$ / $CH_2-CH_2$ | $CH_3-CH_2-CH_2-CH_3$ |
| E | F |
| $CH_3-C=CH_2$ with $CH_3$ below | $CH_2=CH-CH_2-CH_2-CH_3$ |

(a) Identify the isomer(s) of

$$CH_2=CH-CH_2-CH_3$$

| A | B |
|---|---|
| C | D |
| E | F |

(b) Identify the **two** compounds with general formula $C_nH_{2n}$, which do **not** react quickly with bromine solution.

| A | B |
|---|---|
| C | D |
| E | F |

57

**5.** Glucose, sucrose and starch are all carbohydrates.

Identify the correct statement(s).

| | |
|---|---|
| A | Glucose and sucrose are isomers of each other. |
| B | Starch is formed by glucose molecules joining together. |
| C | Sucrose can be hydrolysed to give starch. |
| D | When sucrose is heated with dilute acid, glucose is formed. |
| E | Glucose is formed from carbon dioxide and water during respiration. |
| F | Glucose is an example of a disaccharide. |

| |
|---|
| A |
| B |
| C |
| D |
| E |
| F |

KU PS

**6.** Elements can be classified in different ways.

| A | They are non-metals. |
|---|---|
| B | They are in the same group. |
| C | They form ions with a negative charge. |
| D | They are solids at 25 °C. |
| E | They have the same number of electron shells. |

(a) Identify the statement(s) which can be applied to **both** gallium and bromine.

| A |
|---|
| B |
| C |
| D |
| E |

(b) Identify the statement(s) which can be applied to **both** strontium and barium.

| A |
|---|
| B |
| C |
| D |
| E |

7.  Magnesium phosphide is used in distress flares.

    Identify the correct statement(s).

| A | It has the formula $Mg_2P_3$. |
|---|---|
| B | It is formed from magnesium, phosphorus and oxygen. |
| C | It conducts electricity if it is molten. |
| D | It is made up of molecules. |
| E | It is a solid at room temperature. |

| |
|---|
| A |
| B |
| C |
| D |
| E |

**8.** The table gives information about some atoms.

| Atom | Atomic number | Mass number |
|------|---------------|-------------|
| P | 22 | 50 |
| Q | 24 | 50 |
| R | 24 | 54 |
| S | 26 | 54 |
| T | 26 | 56 |

Identify the correct statement(s).

| | |
|---|---|
| A | Atoms P and Q have the same number of protons. |
| B | Atoms Q and R have the same number of electrons. |
| C | Atoms P and S have the same number of neutrons. |
| D | Atoms R and S are isotopes of each other. |
| E | Atoms S and T have different chemical properties. |

| |
|---|
| A |
| B |
| C |
| D |
| E |

**9.** Identify the statement(s) which can be applied to iron but **not** to copper.

KU PS

| | |
|---|---|
| A | It displaces tin from a solution of tin chloride. |
| B | It reacts with cold water. |
| C | It can be obtained by heating its oxide with carbon. |
| D | It reacts with dilute hydrochloric acid. |
| E | It is displaced from a solution of its chloride by zinc. |

| |
|---|
| A |
| B |
| C |
| D |
| E |

## PART 2

### A total of 40 marks is available in this part of the paper.

**10.** The diagram represents the structure of an atom.

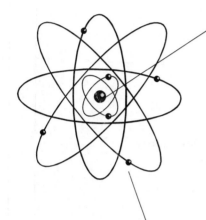

| THE NUCLEUS | | |
|---|---|---|
| Name of particle | Relative mass | Charge |
| PROTON | 1 | (a) |
| NEUTRON | (b) | 0 |

| OUTSIDE THE NUCLEUS | | |
|---|---|---|
| Name of particle | Relative mass | Charge |
| (c) | almost zero | (d) |

Fill in the missing information at (a), (b), (c) and (d) in the tables.    **(2)**

Marks KU PS

**11.** Euan investigated the protection of iron from rusting.

He connected different metals to an iron nail in a cell.

The metals he used were copper, magnesium, tin and zinc.

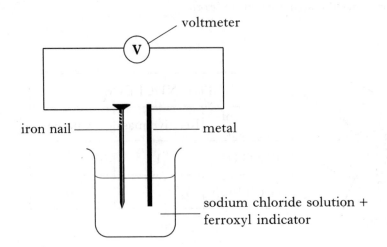

In his table of results, he did not name the metals used.

| Experiment | Blue colour at nail? | Voltage (V) |
|------------|----------------------|-------------|
| 1 | no | 1·9 |
| 2 | yes | 0·7 |
| 3 | no | 0·3 |
| 4 | yes | 0·2 |

Identify the metal used in each experiment.

Experiment 1 _____

Experiment 2 _____

Experiment 3 _____

Experiment 4 _____

(You may wish to use your data booklet, page 7.)　　　　　　(2)

**12.** The graph shows annual sales of leaded and unleaded petrol from 1984 onwards.

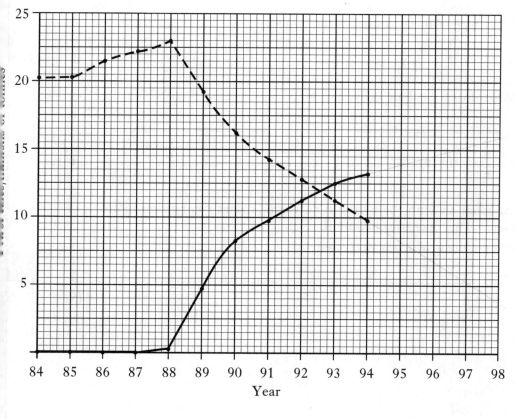

—— unleaded petrol          - - - - leaded petrol

(*a*) Describe the trends in the amounts of leaded and unleaded petrol sold between 1988 and 1994.

_____

_____          **1**

(*b*) Predict the sales of leaded and unleaded petrol for 1998 if these trends continue.

_____

_____          **1**

*Marks*

| KU | PS |
|----|----|

(c) Most modern car exhausts are fitted with a catalytic converter.

    (i) What type of metal is used as the catalyst?

_____  1

    (ii) What does a catalytic converter do?

_____

_____  1

(d) Mixing more air with the petrol in an engine makes combustion more complete. This decreases pollution.

Name a pollutant which is decreased.

_____  1

(5)

**13.** Zinc occurs in the Earth's crust mainly as zinc sulphide, ZnS. The flow chart shows the main steps in extracting the metal.

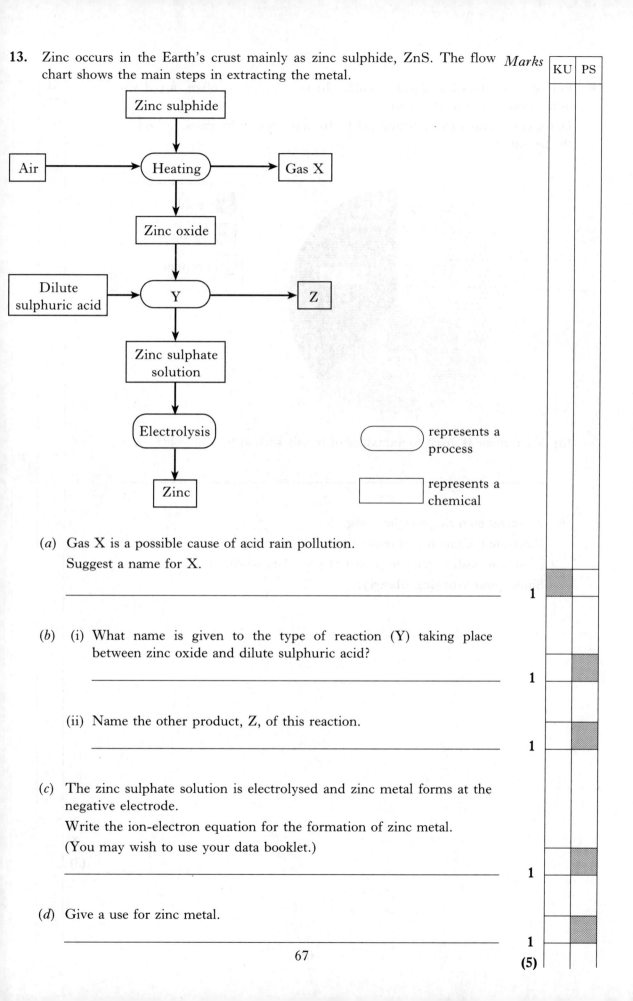

*Marks*

| | KU | PS |
|---|---|---|

(a) Gas X is a possible cause of acid rain pollution.

Suggest a name for X.

_____   1

(b) (i) What name is given to the type of reaction (Y) taking place between zinc oxide and dilute sulphuric acid?

_____   1

(ii) Name the other product, Z, of this reaction.

_____   1

(c) The zinc sulphate solution is electrolysed and zinc metal forms at the negative electrode.

Write the ion-electron equation for the formation of zinc metal.

(You may wish to use your data booklet.)

_____   1

(d) Give a use for zinc metal.

_____   1

(5)

*Marks*  KU  PS

**14.** Pure gold is known as 24-carat gold. In jewellery, it is often mixed with other metals to make it harder.

One common mixture is 9-carat gold. Its composition by mass is shown in the pie-chart.

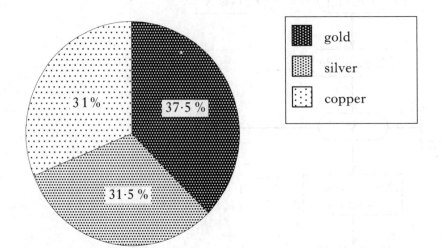

(*a*) What name is given to a mixture of metals such as 9-carat gold?

_____

1

(*b*) A 9-carat gold ring weighs 7·88g.

Calculate the number of moles of gold in the ring.

(You may wish to refer to page 4 of your data booklet.)

**Show your working clearly.**

2

**(3)**

**15.** Common salt is extracted from salt mines by pumping in water to dissolve it.

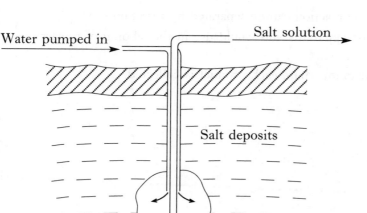

The salt solution which is obtained contains magnesium sulphate as an impurity.

The magnesium ions are removed by adding sodium hydroxide solution.

$$Mg^{2+}(aq) + SO_4^{2-}(aq) + 2Na^+(aq) + 2OH^-(aq) \longrightarrow Mg^{2+}(OH^-)_2(s) + 2Na^+(aq) + SO_4^{2-}(aq)$$

(*a*) (i) Name the type of reaction taking place between the magnesium sulphate solution and the sodium hydroxide solution.

_____   1

  (ii) Name the spectator ions in the reaction.

_____   1

*Marks* | KU | PS

(b) The products of the reaction can be separated by filtration.

Draw and label the apparatus you would use in the laboratory to carry out this process.

Indicate on the diagram where each product is collected.

2

(4)

*Marks*

**16.** The full structural formulae below represent two members of a homologous series of compounds called the cycloalkenes.

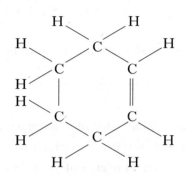

cyclobutene                    cyclohexene

(a) What is the general formula for the cycloalkene series?

_____    1

(b) Draw the full structural formula for the cycloalkene with five carbon atoms.

1

(c) Cyclobutene reacts with bromine solution.

Write the molecular formula for the compound formed.

_____    1

**(3)**

**17.** Nitrogen is used to fill the air-bags which protect people in car crashes. It is produced when sodium azide ($NaN_3$) decomposes rapidly.

$$2NaN_3(s) \longrightarrow 2Na(s) + 3N_2(g)$$

(a) Why is nitrogen a suitable gas for this purpose?

_____

**1**

(b) A driver's air bag contains 60 g of sodium azide.
Calculate the mass of nitrogen gas which will be produced.
(You may wish to refer to page 4 of your data booklet.)
**Show your working clearly.**

**2**

**(3)**

Marks    KU   PS

**18.** Gillian investigated the ability of different substances to conduct electricity when dissolved in water.

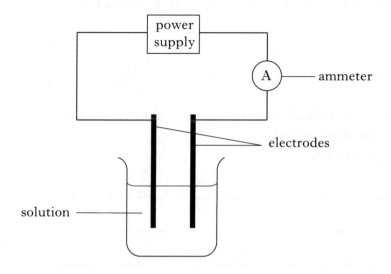

Here are her results.

| Substance | Concentration of solution (mol/l) | Current (mA) |
|---|---|---|
| sodium chloride | 0·005 | 21 |
| sodium chloride | 0·002 | 11 |
| sodium chloride | 0·001 | 7 |
| hydrochloric acid | 0·005 | 62 |
| hydrochloric acid | 0·002 | 27 |
| hydrochloric acid | 0·001 | 20 |
| sodium hydroxide | 0·005 | 32 |
| sodium hydroxide | 0·002 | 15 |
| sodium hydroxide | 0·001 | 11 |

(a) What name is used to describe a solution which conducts electricity?

_____ 1

(b) Identify **two** variables which she would have kept constant to make sure that her results were fair.

_____

_____ 1

*Marks* | KU | PS

(c) From the results, state the effect of changing concentration on the ability of a substance to conduct electricity when dissolved in water.

_____

_____  1

(d) Arrange the three substances in order of their ability to conduct electricity when dissolved in water.

(Put the best conductor first.)

1  _____

2  _____

3  _____  1

(4)

**19.** The OXO Process involves the reaction between an alkene and synthesis gas (a mixture of carbon monoxide and hydrogen).

The product is an alcohol with one carbon atom more than the alkene.

For example,

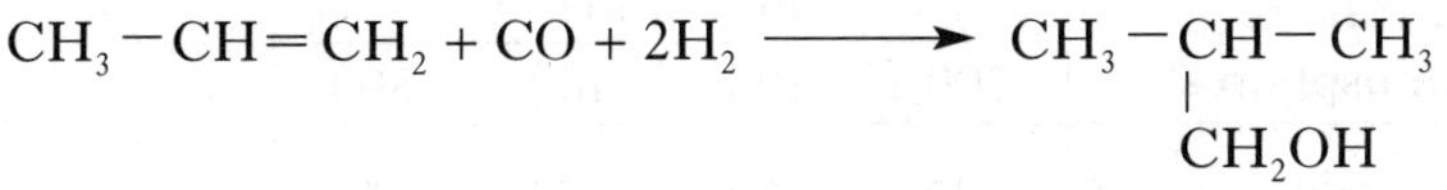

$$CH_3-CH=CH_2 + CO + 2H_2 \longrightarrow CH_3-CH-CH_3$$
$$\mid$$
$$CH_2OH$$

an alcohol

(a) Draw the formula for an alkene which would give the following alcohol.

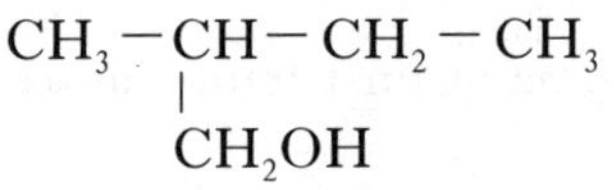

$$CH_3-CH-CH_2-CH_3$$
$$\mid$$
$$CH_2OH$$

**1**

(b) Draw the formula for the alcohol which would be formed from ethene.

**1**

**(2)**

**20.** The table shows the percentage yields of ammonia obtained from nitrogen and hydrogen at various temperatures and pressures.

**Percentage yields of ammonia**

| Pressure/ atmospheres | Temperature/°C | | | |
|---|---|---|---|---|
| | 200 | 300 | 400 | 500 |
| 100 | 82 | 53 | 25 | 11 |
| 200 | 89 | 67 | 39 | 18 |
| 300 | 90 | 71 | 47 | 24 |
| 400 | 95 | 80 | 55 | 32 |

(a) Draw a line graph of percentage yield of ammonia against temperature for a pressure of 200 atmospheres.

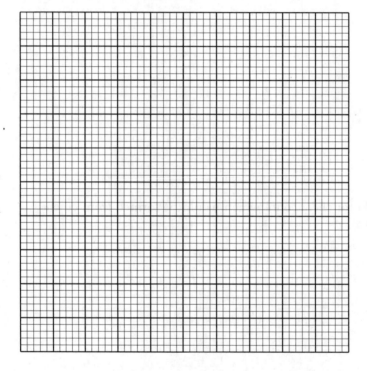

**2**

(b) High yields of ammonia are obtained at low temperatures, but in practice a moderately high temperature is used. Why is this?

_____

_____

**1**

(c) Explain why all of the nitrogen and hydrogen are not converted to ammonia.

_____

_____

**1**

**(4)**

*Marks* | KU | PS

*Marks*  KU  PS

**21.**  Stuart wanted to prepare ammonium sulphate.

He carried out a titration using 0·5 mol/l sulphuric acid and 0·5 mol/l ammonia solution.

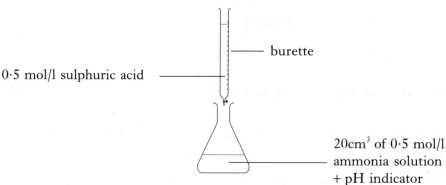

0·5 mol/l sulphuric acid ——————— burette

20cm³ of 0·5 mol/l ammonia solution + pH indicator

The equation for the reaction is

$$2NH_3(aq) + H_2SO_4(aq) \longrightarrow (NH_4)_2SO_4(aq)$$

(a)  Calculate the volume of sulphuric acid Stuart used to neutralise the ammonia solution.

2

(b)  The indicator was removed from the ammonium sulphate solution by filtering the solution through charcoal.

How would Stuart then obtain a sample of solid ammonium sulphate from the solution?

_____

_____

1

(3)

*[END OF QUESTION PAPER]*

SCOTTISH
CERTIFICATE OF
EDUCATION
1998

MONDAY, 18 MAY
11.00 AM – 12.30 PM

CHEMISTRY
STANDARD GRADE
Credit Level

## PART 1

1. Different numbers are used to give information about atoms.

KU | PS

| A | Atomic number |
| B | Mass number |
| C | Number of outer electrons |
| D | Number of electron energy levels |

(a) Identify the number which is the number of protons plus neutrons in an atom.

| A |
| B |
| C |
| D |

(b) Identify the number which is the same for sodium and chlorine atoms.

| A |
| B |
| C |
| D |

**2.** Reactions can be represented using ionic equations.

| A | $H^+(aq) + OH^-(aq) \rightarrow H_2O(\ell)$ |
|---|---|
| B | $2H_2O(\ell) + O_2(g) + 4e \rightarrow 4OH^-(aq)$ |
| C | $2H^+(aq) + CO_3^{2-}(aq) \rightarrow H_2O(\ell) + CO_2(g)$ |
| D | $SO_2(g) + H_2O(\ell) \rightarrow 2H^+(aq) + SO_3^{2-}(aq)$ |
| E | $NH_4^+(s) + OH^-(s) \rightarrow NH_3(g) + H_2O(\ell)$ |

(a) Identify the ionic equation representing reduction.

| A |
|---|
| B |
| C |
| D |
| E |

(b) Identify the ionic equation which shows the formation of acid rain.

| A |
|---|
| B |
| C |
| D |
| E |

(c) Identify the **two** ionic equations which show the neutralisation of an acid.

| A |
|---|
| B |
| C |
| D |
| E |

3. Many compounds contain carbon, hydrogen and oxygen.

| A | $H-C{\Large\substack{\nearrow O \\ \searrow O-H}}$ |
|---|---|
| B | H   H<br>\|   \|<br>H$-$C$-$C$-$O$-$H<br>\|   \|<br>H   H |
| C | H<br>\|<br>H$-$C$-$C${\Large\substack{\nearrow O \\ \searrow H}}$<br>\|<br>H |
| D | H       H<br>\|       \|<br>H$-$C$-$O$-$C$-$H<br>\|       \|<br>H       H |
| E | H   H       H<br>\|   \|       \|<br>H$-$C$-$C$-$O$-$C$-$H<br>\|   \|       \|<br>H   H       H |

(a) Identify the **two** compounds which have the same molecular formula.

| A |
|---|
| B |
| C |
| D |
| E |

(b) Identify the compound which has the general formula $C_nH_{2n}O$.

| A |
|---|
| B |
| C |
| D |
| E |

**4.** The chemical processes in the grid involve catalysts.

KU PS

| A | Haber Process |
| B | Ostwald Process |
| C | Hydrolysis of starch |
| D | Cracking of hydrocarbons |
| E | Formation of alkanes from alkenes |

(a) Identify the process in which the catalyst can be an enzyme.

| A |
| B |
| C |
| D |
| E |

(b) Identify the process(es) in which hydrogen gas is a reactant.

| A |
| B |
| C |
| D |
| E |

**5.** Manganese dioxide acts as a catalyst in the breakdown of hydrogen peroxide solution.

$$2H_2O_2(aq) \rightarrow 2H_2O(\ell) + O_2(g)$$

hydrogen peroxide

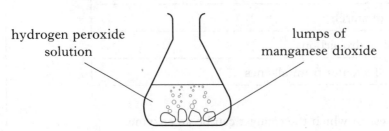

hydrogen peroxide solution

lumps of manganese dioxide

| A | Heating the solution |
| B | Powdering the manganese dioxide |
| C | Increasing the volume of the solution |
| D | Increasing the concentration of the solution |

(a) Identify the change which would **not** increase the rate of the reaction.

| A |
| B |
| C |
| D |

(b) Identify the change(s) in condition which would increase the mass of oxygen produced.

| A |
| B |
| C |
| D |

KU  PS

**6.** There are many different chemical reactions.

| A addition | B cracking | C displacement |
|---|---|---|
| D neutralisation | E polymerisation | F precipitation |

(*a*) Identify the reaction which produces starch from glucose.

| A | B | C |
|---|---|---|
| D | E | F |

(*b*) Identify the type(s) of reaction represented by the following equation.

$$Ba(OH)_2(aq) + H_2SO_4(aq) \rightarrow BaSO_4(s) + 2H_2O(\ell)$$

| A | B | C |
|---|---|---|
| D | E | F |

**7.** It is important to protect iron from rusting.

Identify the correct statement(s) about the rusting of iron.

| A | Copper gives sacrificial protection to iron. |
|---|---|
| B | Ferroxyl indicator turns pink in the presence of $Fe^{2+}$ ions. |
| C | Electroplating provides a surface barrier to air and water. |
| D | Tin plated iron rusts quickly when the coating is scratched. |
| E | Iron rusts when attached to the negative terminal of a battery. |

| |
|---|
| A |
| B |
| C |
| D |
| E |

KU PS

**8.** The lowest temperature at which a hydrocarbon ignites is called its flash point.

| Hydrocarbon | Formula | Boiling point/°C | Flash point/°C |
|---|---|---|---|
| hexene | $C_6H_{12}$ | 64 | −9 |
| hexane | $C_6H_{14}$ | 68 | −21 |
| cyclohexane | $C_6H_{12}$ | 81 | −21 |
| heptane | $C_7H_{16}$ | 98 | −4 |
| octane | $C_8H_{18}$ | 126 | 13 |

Identify the correct statement(s).

| | |
|---|---|
| A | Octane will **not** ignite at 0 °C. |
| B | Isomers have the same flash point. |
| C | The flash points of hydrocarbons increase as the boiling points increase. |
| D | In a homologous series the flash point increases as the number of carbon atoms increases. |

| |
|---|
| A |
| B |
| C |
| D |

*Marks*

## PART 2

### A total of 40 marks is available in this part of the paper.

9.  $^{14}_{6}C$ is an isotope of carbon. It occurs naturally in carbon dioxide and is present in plants as a result of photosynthesis.

(a) What are isotopes?

_____

_____

_____

_____    1

(b) Complete the table to show the numbers of protons, neutrons and electrons in an atom of $^{14}_{6}C$.

| Particle | Number |
|----------|--------|
| protons | |
| neutrons | |
| electrons | |

   1

(c) Sunlight is essential for photosynthesis. Name the substance in green plants which can absorb sunlight.

_____    1

**(3)**

*Marks*

| | KU | PS |
|---|---|---|

**10.** In a chlorine molecule the atoms share two electrons in a covalent bond.

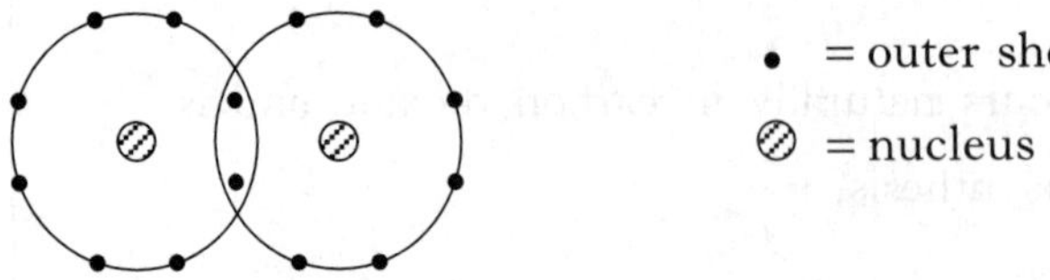

• = outer shell electron

⊘ = nucleus

(*a*) Explain how the chlorine atoms are held together in a chlorine molecule.

_____

_____

_____

_____    **1**

(*b*) (i) Chlorine forms a solid ionic compound with potassium.
Chloride ions have a stable electron arrangement.
How do they achieve this arrangement?

_____

_____

_____

_____    **1**

(ii) Explain why ionic compounds are solid.

_____

_____

_____    **1**

**(3)**

*Marks*

KU | PS

**11.** Zinc reacts with copper sulphate solution.

$$Zn(s) + Cu^{2+}(aq) + SO_4^{2-}(aq) \rightarrow Zn^{2+}(aq) + SO_4^{2-}(aq) + Cu(s)$$

(*a*) Rewrite the equation omitting the spectator ions.

_____

1

(*b*)

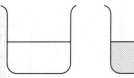 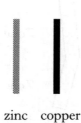   

zinc sulphate    copper sulphate    zinc   copper    connecting    voltmeter    salt bridge
solution       solution                 wires

Draw a **labelled** diagram in the space below to show how **all** of the pieces of apparatus shown can be used to make a cell.

2

(3)

*Marks*

| | | KU | PS |

**12.** Iron is made in a blast furnace by the reduction of iron oxide.

| Zone | Main reaction |
|------|---------------|
| 3 | $Fe_2O_3(s) + CO(g) \rightarrow Fe(s) + CO_2(g)$ |
| 2 | $CO_2(G) + C(s) \rightarrow 2CO(g)$ |
| 1 | $C(s) + O_2(g) \rightarrow CO_2(g)$ |

iron ore, carbon
and limestone

waste
gases

Zone 3

Zone 2

Zone 1

air →          ← air

SLAG

slag ←

IRON

→ iron

(a) Why is air blown into the furnace?

_____

_____

_____

_____          1

(b) Both carbon and carbon monoxide can reduce iron oxide.
Why is carbon monoxide a more effective reducing agent than carbon?

_____

_____

_____

_____          1

*Marks*

| KU | PS |
|----|----|

(c) Rewrite the equation for the main reaction in zone 3 as a balanced equation.

_____    **1**


(d) Iron ore is a mixture of compounds. One of these is called siderite and has the composition:

       iron             48·3 %
       oxygen      41·4 %
       carbon     10·3 %

Calculate the empirical formula of siderite.
**Show your working clearly.**

**2**

**(5)**

**13.** Silver oxide cells are used in calculators and watches.

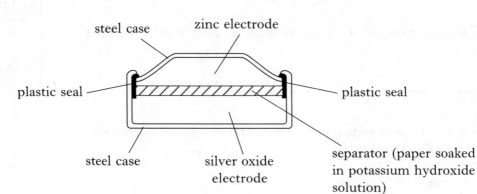

steel case    zinc electrode

plastic seal    plastic seal

steel case    silver oxide electrode    separator (paper soaked in potassium hydroxide solution)

Marks  KU  PS

(a) (i) How is electricity produced in a cell?

_____

_____

_____ 1

(ii) Give a disadvantage of a cell.

_____

_____

_____ 1

(b) The equation shows the reaction which takes place at the zinc electrode.

$$Zn(s) + 2(OH)^-(aq) \rightarrow ZnO(s) + H_2O_{(\ell)} + 2e$$

State why the equation represents oxidation.

_____

_____ 1

(c) Why has the separator been soaked in potassium hydroxide solution?

_____

_____ 1

**(4)**

*Marks*

**14.** Haloalkanes are alkane molecules with a hydrogen atom replaced by a halogen atom.

The name of the haloalkane depends on the position of the halogen atom in the molecule.

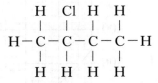

1-chlorobutane                    2-chlorobutane

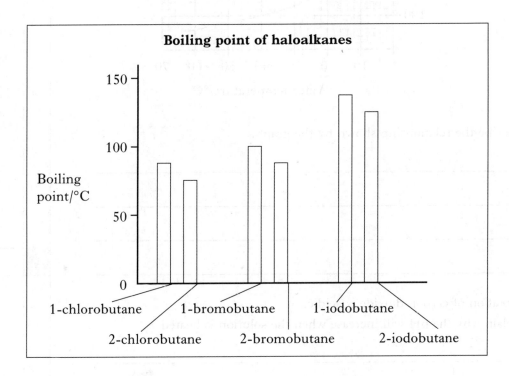

Describe **two** trends shown by the information in the bar chart.

1 _____

_____

_____

2 _____

_____

_____

(2)

KU | PS

*Marks*

KU | PS

**15.** The graph shows the relationship between the solubility of carbon dioxide in water and the temperature of the water.

### Solubility of Carbon Dioxide

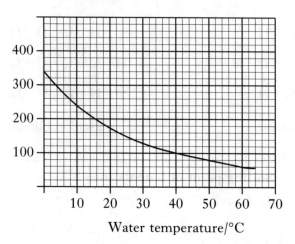

Solubility of carbon dioxide/ mg per 100 g

Water temperature/°C

(a) Describe the relationship shown by the graph.

_____

_____

_____

_____     **1**

(b) A solution of carbon dioxide is acidic.
Explain why the pH will increase when the solution is heated.

_____

_____

_____

_____     **1**

**(2)**

*Marks*

**16.** Ammonium compounds can be identified by heating them with soda lime. This produces ammonia.

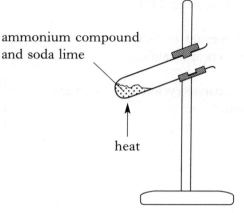

ammonium compound and soda lime

heat

(a) What type of compound is soda lime?

_____     1

(b) Give a test which would detect ammonia at the mouth of the test tube.

_____

_____

_____     1

(c) An ammonium compound was dissolved in water.

A precipitate was produced when this solution was added to a solution of barium chloride.

Suggest a name for the compound.

(You may wish to use page 5 in the data booklet to help you.)

_____     1

                                                   **(3)**

| KU | PS |
|----|----|

*Marks*

**17.**                     **Preparation of cyclohexene**

| KU | PS |

$$\text{cyclohexanol} \quad \rightarrow \quad \text{cyclohexene} + \text{water}$$

boiling point 161 °C             boiling point 83 °C

**Stage 1**     Cyclohexanol is heated for 20 minutes at 70 °C. Concentrated phosphoric acid acts as a catalyst.

**Stage 2**     The temperature is raised to separate cyclohexene from the reaction mixture by distillation.

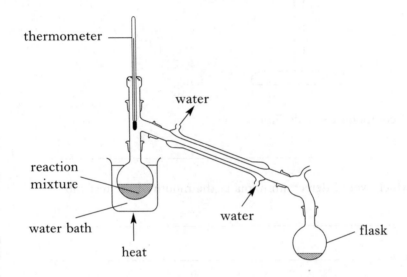

(a) Name the substances in the reaction mixture at the start of the reaction.

_____

_____    **1**

(b) What ensures a fast rate of reaction at Stage 1?

_____

_____

_____    **1**

(c) Why does **no** liquid collect in the flask during Stage 1?

_____

_____

_____    **1**

*Marks*

| | KU | PS |
|---|---|---|

(*d*) Why is it possible to separate cyclohexene from the reaction mixture at Stage 2?

_____

_____

_____ **1**

**(4)**

18. Silver nitrate solution can be used to determine the mass of chloride ions in 1 litre of sea water.

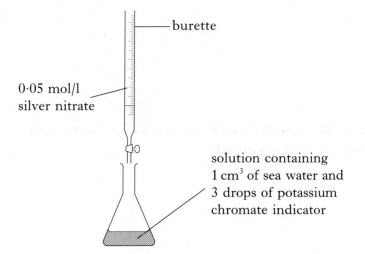

burette

0·05 mol/l
silver nitrate

solution containing
1 cm³ of sea water and
3 drops of potassium
chromate indicator

Volume of silver nitrate solution used to reach the end-point = $10\cdot8\,cm^3$.

(*a*) (i) How many moles of silver nitrate does $10\cdot8\,cm^3$ of $0\cdot05$ mol/l silver nitrate solution contain?
   **Show your working clearly.**

**1**

*Marks*

| KU | PS |
|---|---|

(ii) One mole of silver nitrate solution reacts with one mole of chloride ions.

How many moles of chloride ions are there in 1 litre of the sea water?

**Show your working clearly.**

1

(iii) Calculate the mass of chloride ions in 1 litre of the sea water.

**Show your working clearly.**

1

(b) The end point of the titration is indicated by the formation of red silver(I) chromate.

Write the formula for silver(I) chromate.

_____

1

(4)

*Marks*

KU | PS

**19.** Ethylene glycol is used as an antifreeze in car radiators.

It is made from ethene in two steps.

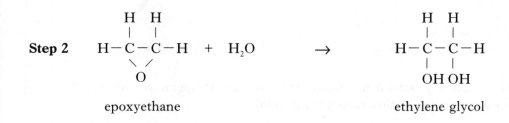

**Step 1**

$$C = C \ (ethene) + O_2 \xrightarrow{\text{silver catalyst}} \text{epoxyethane}$$

**Step 2**    epoxyethane + $H_2O$ → ethylene glycol

(*a*) Name the type of reaction in Step 1.

_____    1

(*b*) Salt could also act as an antifreeze but would cause rusting in the radiator.

Why does ethylene glycol not cause rusting?

_____

_____

_____    1

(*c*) In Step 2, epoxyethane reacts with water.

Epoxyethane can also react with hydrogen.

Draw the structural formula of the substance which would be produced.

1

(3)

*Marks*

**20.** Paul investigated temperature changes during displacement reactions. KU | PS

He added excess magnesium powder to $25\,cm^3$ of each solution and recorded the change in temperature.

| Solution | Temperature/°C | |
|---|---|---|
| | Initial | Final |
| copper chloride | 25 | 67 |
| nickel chloride | 25 | 49 |
| iron chloride | 25 | 44 |
| zinc chloride | 25 | 39 |
| magnesium chloride | 25 | |

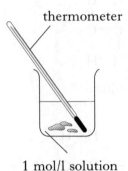

thermometer

1 mol/l solution

(a) Write a general statement about the rise in temperature when magnesium displaces other metals from solutions.

_____

_____

_____ 1

(b) Add to the table the final temperature you would expect Paul to have found when magnesium chloride solution was used. 1

(c) State **two** ways in which Paul ensured that the investigation was fair.

1 _____

_____

2 _____

_____ 1

(d) What other evidence for a chemical reaction would have been seen when magnesium was added to copper chloride solution?

_____

_____

_____ 1

**(4)**

*[END OF QUESTION PAPER]*

**PART 1**

KU | PS

1. The table gives information about some substances.

| Substance | Melting point/°C | Boiling point/°C | Conducts as | |
|:---:|:---:|:---:|:---:|:---:|
| | | | a solid | a liquid |
| A | 1890 | 3380 | yes | yes |
| B | 963 | 1560 | no | yes |
| C | 1455 | 2730 | yes | yes |
| D | −183 | −164 | no | no |
| E | 1700 | 2230 | no | no |
| F | 712 | 1418 | no | yes |

(a) Identify the **two** ionic compounds.

| A |
|---|
| B |
| C |
| D |
| E |
| F |

(b) Identify the covalent molecular compound.

| A |
|---|
| B |
| C |
| D |
| E |
| F |

| | KU | PS |
|---|---|---|

**2.** Carbohydrates are formed in plants.

| A | fructose |
|---|---|
| B | glucose |
| C | maltose |
| D | starch |
| E | sucrose |

(a) Identify the carbohydrate which does not dissolve well in water.

| A |
|---|
| B |
| C |
| D |
| E |

(b) Identify the **two** carbohydrates with the formula $C_{12}H_{22}O_{11}$.

| A |
|---|
| B |
| C |
| D |
| E |

(c) Identify the carbohydrate which is a condensation polymer.

| A |
|---|
| B |
| C |
| D |
| E |

| KU | PS |
|----|----|

(d) Identify the **two** carbohydrates which **cannot** be hydrolysed.

| A |
|---|
| B |
| C |
| D |
| E |

3. Precipitation reactions can be used to prepare some salts.

| A copper nitrate | B barium sulphate |
|---|---|
| C lithium carbonate | D sodium chloride |

You may wish to refer to page 5 of the data booklet to help you with both parts.

(a) Identify the salt which can be prepared by a precipitation reaction.

| A | B |
|---|---|
| C | D |

(b) Identify the **two** soluble salts whose solutions would form a precipitate when mixed.

| A | B |
|---|---|
| C | D |

KU | PS

4.  Iron and magnesium both react with dilute hydrochloric acid.

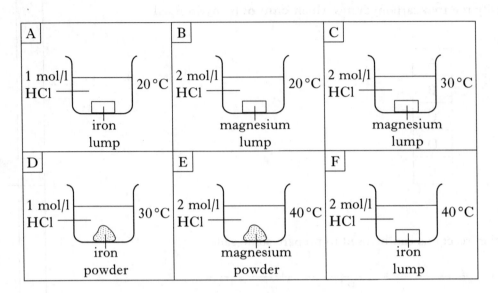

(a)  Identify the experiment with the **slowest** rate of reaction.

| A | B | C |
|---|---|---|
| D | E | F |

(b)  Identify the **two** experiments which could be used to investigate the effect of temperature on the rate of reaction.

| A | B | C |
|---|---|---|
| D | E | F |

| | KU | PS |
|---|---|---|

**5.** Nuclide notation allows the numbers of electrons, protons and neutrons in **atoms** and **ions** to be calculated.

| A | B | C |
|---|---|---|
| $^{23}_{11}Na$ | $^{39}_{19}K^+$ | $^{37}_{17}Cl^-$ |
| D | E | F |
| $^{24}_{11}Na$ | $^{39}_{19}K$ | $^{35}_{17}Cl$ |

(a) Identify the **two atoms** which are isotopes.

| A | B | C |
|---|---|---|
| D | E | F |

(b) Identify the **two** particles with the same electron arrangements as argon.

| A | B | C |
|---|---|---|
| D | E | F |

(c) Identify the particle with 18 neutrons.

| A | B | C |
|---|---|---|
| D | E | F |

**6.** When two different metals are joined in a cell, a chemical reaction takes place and a voltage is produced.

During the reaction one of the metals corrodes.

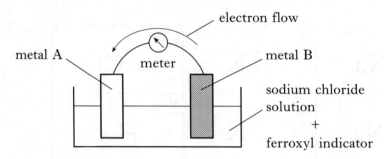

| | Metal A | Metal B |
|---|---|---|
| A | lead | zinc |
| B | iron | nickel |
| C | nickel | lead |
| D | lead | iron |
| E | zinc | iron |

(a) Which pair of metals would produce a flow of electrons in the same direction as shown in the diagram **and** produce a blue colour round metal B?

| A |
|---|
| B |
| C |
| D |
| E |

(b) Which pair of metals would produce the biggest voltage?

You may wish to refer to page 7 of the data booklet to help you.

| A |
|---|
| B |
| C |
| D |
| E |

KU  PS

**7.** Mr Sharp demonstrated the fractional distillation of crude oil to class 3B.

KU | PS

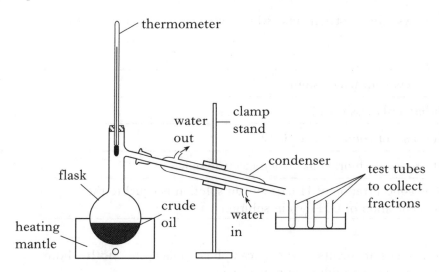

He collected six fractions and numbered them according to the order in which they were collected.

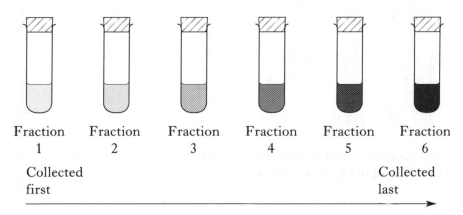

| Fraction 1 | Fraction 2 | Fraction 3 | Fraction 4 | Fraction 5 | Fraction 6 |

Collected first

Collected last

Identify the true statement(s).

| A | Fraction 6 evaporates most easily. |
|---|---|
| B | Fraction 4 is more viscous then fraction 3. |
| C | Fraction 2 is more flammable than fraction 1. |
| D | Fraction 5 has a lower boiling range than fraction 4. |
| E | The molecules in fraction 3 are larger than those in fraction 2. |

| A |
|---|
| B |
| C |
| D |
| E |

| | KU | PS |
|---|---|---|

**8.** The grid shows some statements which can be applied to different solutions.

| A | It reacts with magnesium. |
|---|---|
| B | It has a pH less than 7. |
| C | It does not conduct electricity. |
| D | It produces chlorine gas when electrolysed. |
| E | The concentration of $H^+(aq)$ ions in solution is equal to the concentration of $OH^-(aq)$ in solution. |

(a) Identify the statement(s) which can be applied to **both** dilute hydrochloric acid and dilute sulphuric acid.

| A |
|---|
| B |
| C |
| D |
| E |

(b) Identify the statement which can be applied to sodium chloride solution but **not** to dilute hydrochloric acid.

| A |
|---|
| B |
| C |
| D |
| E |

| | *Marks* | KU | PS |
|---|---|---|---|

## PART 2

### A total of 40 marks is available in this part of the paper.

**9.** The spike graph shows the relative sizes of some atoms.

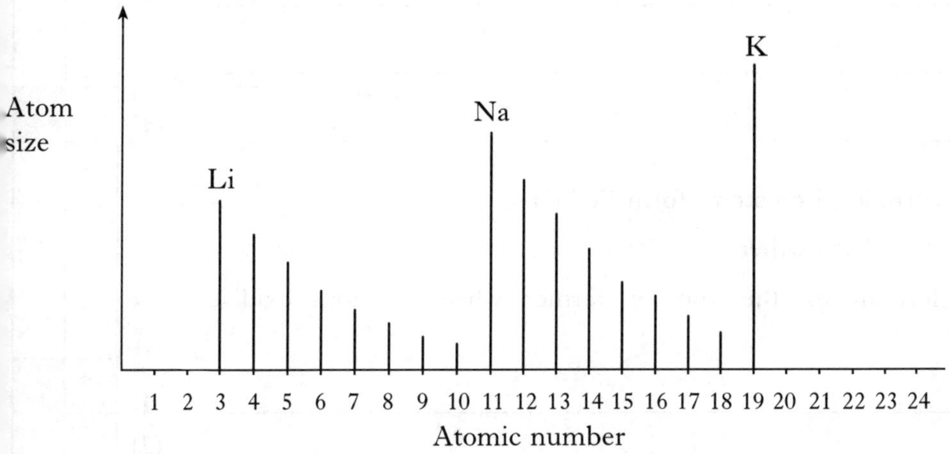

(a) Describe what happens to the atom size going down a group.

_____

_____

_____

_____  **1**

(b) Describe the trend in atom size going from lithium to fluorine.

_____

_____

_____  **1**

(c) Draw a spike on the graph to show the atom size you would expect for calcium.  **1**

**(3)**

Marks | KU | PS

**10.** Many chemical reactions involve atoms either gaining or losing electrons.

    (*a*) Why do atoms gain or lose electrons during reactions?

_____

_____

_____

_____    1

    (*b*) When iron corrodes, iron atoms form $Fe^{2+}$ ions.

         $Fe^{2+}$ ions can oxidise further.

         Write the formula for the iron ion formed when $Fe^{2+}$ ions oxidise further.

_____    1

                                                                   **(2)**

**11.** The two compounds drawn below are added to natural gas to give a smell.

                                                             H
                                                             |

      H      H   H                   H   H−C−H

      |       |    |                     |       |

H−C−S−C−C−H         H−C————C−S−H

      |       |    |                     |       |

      H      H   H                   H       H

           A                                       B

    (*a*) Write the molecular formula for compound A.

_____    1

    (*b*) Why can compound B be described as an isomer of compound A?

_____

_____    1

    (*c*) Name the products formed when these compounds are completely burned in a plentiful supply of oxygen.

_____    1

                                                                         **(3)**

*Marks* | KU | PS

**12.** When chlorine gas is prepared in a fume cupboard it contains acid fumes.

The chlorine gas is bubbled through water to remove the acid fumes. It is then bubbled through concentrated sulphuric acid to dry the gas. The dried gas is collected in a gas jar.

Complete and label the diagram to show how a sample of dry gas could be obtained.

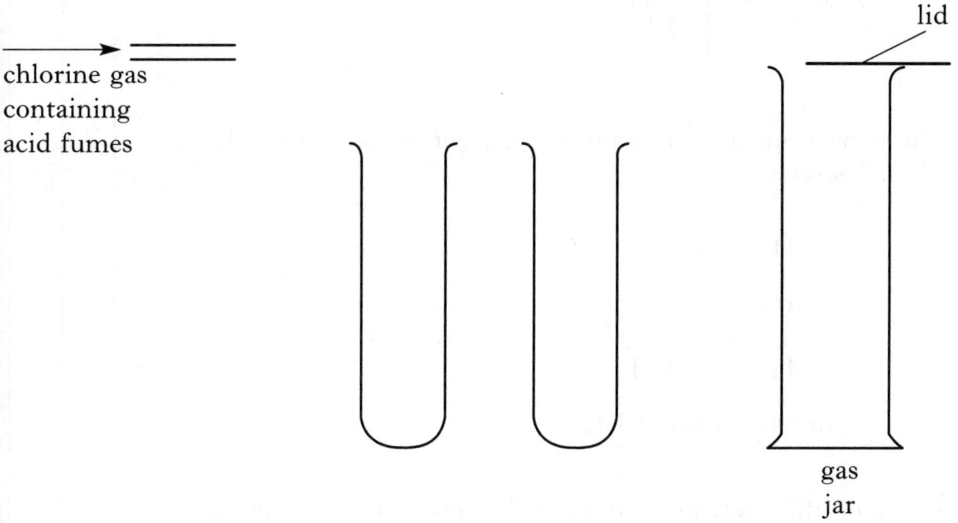

lid

chlorine gas
containing
acid fumes

gas
jar

(2)

*Marks* | KU | PS

**13.** During hip replacement operations the new hip joint is fixed in place using bone cement.

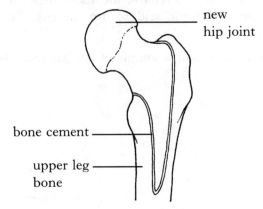

new hip joint

bone cement

upper leg bone

The most popular bone cement is a synthetic polymer formed from the monomer methyl methacrylate.

$$\begin{array}{ccc} H & & CH_3 \\ | & & | \\ C & = & C \\ | & & | \\ H & & COOCH_3 \end{array}$$

methyl methacrylate

(a) Draw a section of this polymer, showing 3 monomer units joined together.

1

(b) As the polymer forms, it releases large amounts of heat which can damage surrounding bone.

What term is used to describe a reaction releasing heat?

_____

1

(c) Calculate the percentage of carbon in methyl methacrylate.

2

**(4)**

*Marks* | KU | PS

**14.**

d.c. power supply
+ −

electrodes

dilute
hydrochloric
acid

dilute sodium
hydroxide
solution

**green** gel containing potassium nitrate
and **universal indicator**

The migration of ions was studied using the apparatus above.

(a) Suggest why potassium nitrate is added to the gel.

_____

_____

_____ **1**

(b) During the experiment, colour changes were observed in the gel.

d.c. power supply
+ −

dilute
hydrochloric
acid

dilute sodium
hydroxide
solution

red
colour

purple
colour

green

Explain, in terms of the migration of ions, the colour changes observed.

_____

_____

_____

_____ **2**

**(3)**

*Marks* | KU | PS

**15.** A silver spoon will gradually tarnish if left in air. This is due to the formation of silver sulphide.

(*a*) Balance the equation.

$$Ag(s) \quad + \quad O_2(g) \quad + \quad H_2S(g) \quad \rightarrow \quad Ag_2S(s) \quad + \quad H_2O(\ell)$$

1

(*b*) The silver ions in the silver sulphide tarnish can be converted back to silver atoms by placing the spoon in an aluminium dish containing a solution of baking soda.

tarnished silver spoon 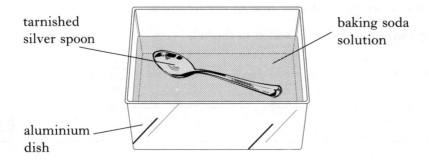 baking soda solution

aluminium dish

(i) Write an ion electron equation for the formation of silver.

1

(ii) Name this type of reaction.

_____ 1

**(3)**

*Marks* | KU | PS

**16.** Alkanols are molecules with one or more hydroxyl (OH) groups.

| *Alkanol* | *Density* g/cm$^3$ |
|---|---|
| OH<br>&#124;<br>H−C−H<br>&#124;<br>H | 0·8 |
| H  OH<br>&#124;  &#124;<br>H−C−C−H<br>&#124;  &#124;<br>H  H | 0·8 |
| OH OH<br>&#124;  &#124;<br>H−C−C−H<br>&#124;  &#124;<br>H  H | 1·1 |
| H  H  OH<br>&#124;  &#124;  &#124;<br>H−C−C−C−H<br>&#124;  &#124;  &#124;<br>H  H  H | 0·8 |
| OH OH OH<br>&#124;  &#124;  &#124;<br>H−C−C−C−H<br>&#124;  &#124;  &#124;<br>H  H  H | 1·3 |

(a) Predict the density of the following alkanol.

$$
\begin{array}{cccc}
H & H & H & OH \\
| & | & | & | \\
H-C-C-C-C-H \\
| & | & | & | \\
H & H & H & H
\end{array}
$$

_____  1

(b) Draw the structural formula of an alkanol with four carbons which would have a density greater than 1·3 g/cm$^3$.

1

(2)

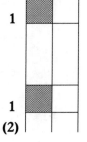

*Marks* | KU | PS

**17.** Nitrogen is important for healthy plant growth.

Most plants obtain the nitrogen they need from compounds of ammonia and nitrates in the soil.

(*a*) Why can plants not use the nitrogen directly from the air?

_____

_____   1

(*b*) Name a substance which would produce ammonia when heated with ammonium chloride.

_____   1

(*c*) During the Ostwald process, ammonia is oxidised to form nitrogen dioxide using a platinum catalyst.

Why is it not necessary to continue heating once the reaction has started?

_____

_____

_____   1

(*d*)

$$H-\overset{\displaystyle N\cdots\cdots H}{\underset{\displaystyle H}{|}} \qquad CH_3-\overset{\displaystyle N\cdots\cdots H}{\underset{\displaystyle H}{|}}$$

      ammonia               methylamine

Ammonia and methylamine share many properties. Both have a strong smell and are soluble in water. Solutions of both substances have a pH greater than 7.

Suggest why ammonia and methylamine have similar properties.

_____

_____

_____   1

  **(4)**

Marks | KU | PS

**18.** The temperature scale shows the melting points of three compounds.

```
50  ─┤
     │
 0  ─┤←──── nitrogen dioxide
     │
-50 ─┤
     │←──── sulphur dioxide
     │←──── ammonia
-100─┤
     │
     ○
```

**melting points °C**

(a) Use the information on page 6 of the data booklet to help you complete a temperature scale showing the **boiling points** of the above compounds.

```
50  ─┤
     │
 0  ─┤
     │
-50 ─┤
     │
     │
-100─┤
     │
     ○
```

**boiling points °C**

1

(b) Name the compound which is liquid at −25 °C.

_____

1

**(2)**

*Marks* | KU | PS

**19.** (*a*) Platinum metal is extracted from its ores using heat alone.

What does this indicate about the reactivity of platinum?

_____

_____

_____  **1**

(*b*) Platinum ores also contain copper sulphide.

When the ores are heated, the copper sulphide reacts to give sulphur dioxide gas.

$$2CuS \; + \; 3O_2 \; \rightarrow \; 2CuO \; + \; 2SO_2$$

Calculate the mass of sulphur dioxide produced when 96 g of copper sulphide is heated.

**2**

(*c*) Some petrol engined cars use catalytic converters containing platinum.

What is the purpose of a catalytic converter?

_____

_____

_____  **1**

**(4)**

*Marks* | KU | PS

**20.** Urea (NH$_2$CONH$_2$) solution is broken down when the enzyme urease is added to it. During the reaction, ammonia and carbon dioxide are produced.

$$NH_2CONH_2 \,(aq) + H_2O(\ell) \quad \rightarrow \quad 2NH_3(aq) + CO_2(g)$$
$$\text{Urea}$$

(*a*) What is an enzyme?

_____ **1**

(*b*) The enzyme activity can be determined by removing a sample from the solution and measuring the concentration of ammonia.

Suggest how the concentration of ammonia could be found.

_____

_____

_____

_____

_____ **1**

(*c*) Enzyme activity was determined at different temperatures.

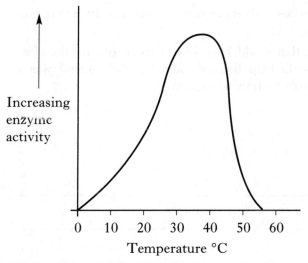

Increasing enzyme activity

Temperature °C

What effect does increasing temperature have on the activity of the enzyme?

_____

_____ **1**

**(3)**

*Marks* | KU | PS

**21.** Pupils in a class were trying to show that a green mineral in a rock was a copper ore.

Firstly they reacted the rock with sulphuric acid.

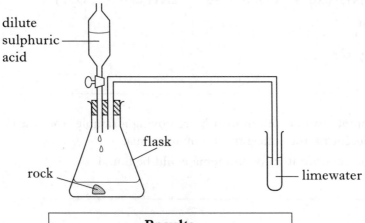

dilute sulphuric acid

flask

rock

limewater

**Results**

(i) Blue solution formed in flask
(ii) Limewater turns milky

(a) During the experiment, the limewater turned milky.

Which **ion** does this indicate is present in the mineral?

_____ 1

(b) The class carried out a second experiment using the blue solution formed in the flask.

Describe an experiment that could have been carried out by the class and explain how this could help them decide that the mineral was a copper ore. (You may wish to draw a diagram.)

_____

_____

_____

_____

_____ 2

(3)

Marks | KU | PS

**22.** A pupil carried out a titration and recorded her results in her jotter.

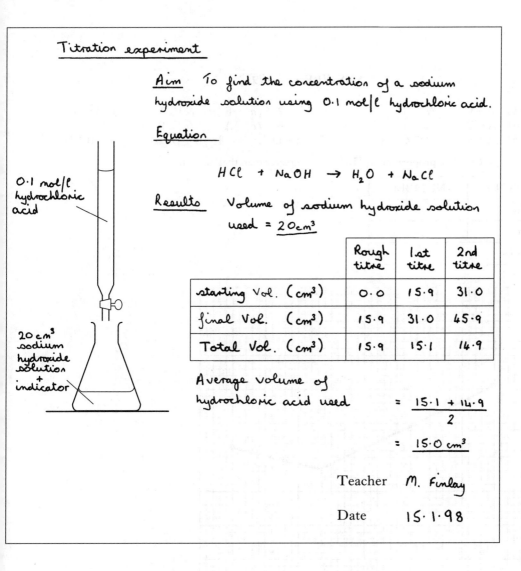

Titration experiment

Aim   To find the concentration of a sodium hydroxide solution using 0.1 mol/ℓ hydrochloric acid.

Equation

$$HCl + NaOH \rightarrow H_2O + NaCl$$

Results   Volume of sodium hydroxide solution used = 20 cm³

|  | Rough titre | 1st titre | 2nd titre |
|---|---|---|---|
| starting Vol. (cm³) | 0.0 | 15.9 | 31.0 |
| final Vol. (cm³) | 15.9 | 31.0 | 45.9 |
| Total Vol. (cm³) | 15.9 | 15.1 | 14.9 |

Average volume of hydrochloric acid used   $= \dfrac{15.1 + 14.9}{2}$

$= 15.0 \text{ cm}^3$

Teacher   M. Finlay

Date   15.1.98

0.1 mol/ℓ hydrochloric acid

20 cm³ sodium hydroxide solution + indicator

Use the pupil's results to calculate the concentration of the sodium hydroxide solution.

(2)

*[END OF QUESTION PAPER]*

1.  *(a)* E    *(b)* A + D    *(c)* C                    2.  *(a)* C + D    *(b)* A + B    *(c)* D + E
3.  *(a)* D    *(b)* E    *(c)* C                        4.  *(a)* C + F    *(b)* A + D    *(c)* E
5.  *(a)* C    *(b)* A + F        6.  B + D             7.  B + F        8.  A + D

## ANSWERS — 1995

1.  *(a)* D    *(b)* A + C    *(c)* D                    2.  *(a)* F    *(b)* A    *(c)* D + E
3.  *(a)* F    *(b)* A + E                               4.  *(a)* A    *(b)* B + C
5.  *(a)* C    *(b)* A + E        6.  B        7.  A + D        8.  A + D        9.  B + D
10. *(a)* Isotopes        *(b)* The proportion of $^{7}_{3}$Li is much greater than that of $^{6}_{3}$Li.

| PARTICLE | NUMBER |
|----------|--------|
| protons | 3 |
| neutrons | 4 |
| electrons | 2 |

11. *(a)*                                                                                     *(b)*  37%

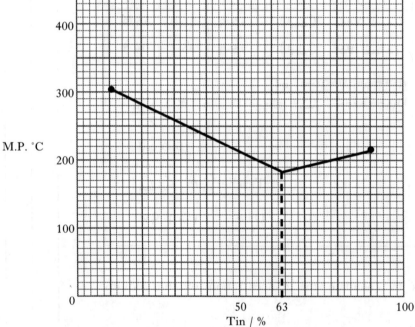

*(c)* Because alloys (often) have more useful properties (of some kind) than the individual metals.
*(d)* Because lead is poisonous.

12. *(a)* (i) Decomposition of an electrolyte by the passage of an electric current.
        (ii) Because the ions of which it is composed are not mobile.
    *(b)* $2\,Cl^{-}\,(aq) \rightarrow Cl^{2}\,(g) + 2\,e^{-}$        *(c)* The pH decreases.

(a) In order to break down the starch and bring it into solution so that the products can pass through the gut wall.

(b) Because glucose can be used immediately for respiration while starch has first to be hydrolysed to glucose.

Set two tubes in a rack.
Add equal volumes of acid to each. Select two zinc lumps of same size and add one to each tube.
Add a few drops of copper sulphate solution to one tube only.
Compare rates of evolution of hydrogen.

(a) To replace soil nutrients that are removed when farm produce is removed and consumed elsewhere; to allow farmers to produce enough food for the very large world population.

(b) It is cheaper to make nitrogen dioxide from ammonia.

(c) Once started, the reactions sustains itself.

(d) Mass of 1 mol of urea $\quad = [(4 \times 1) + (2 \times 14) + 12 + 16]\,g = 60\,g$

Mass of nitrogen in 1 mol $\quad = (2 \times 14)\,g = 28\,g$

$\qquad$ % nitrogen $\quad = \dfrac{28}{60} \times 100\% = 46 \cdot 7\%$

(e) This is a polymer that sets permanently to a solid and cannot be resoftened by heating.

(a) A polymer formed by the joining of unsaturated monomers without loss of material.

(b)
```
H    Cl
|    |
C  = C
|    |
H    Cl
```
(c) May produce poinsonous gases

(d) These polymers do not rot and decay.

(a) Substances dissolve faster in warm water than in cold water.

(b) Formula: NaOH
1 mol has mass of 40 g
1 litre contains 80 g
Amount in mol per litre is 2 mol
Concentration is 2 mol/$L$

(c) 20 cm$^3$ sodium sulphide solution makes 100 cm$^3$ toner
1000 cm$^3$ sodium sulphide solution contains 100 g sodium sulphide

20 cm$^2$ sodium sulphide solution contains $\dfrac{100}{1000} \times 20$ g sodium sulphide = 2 g sodium sulphide

(a) Butane $\qquad$ (b) Iodomethane and iodoethane

(c)
```
   H   H   H   H
   |   |   |   |
I— C — C — C — C — I
   |   |   |   |
   H   H   H   H
```

(a) Covalent discrete molecular

(b) (1) $2H_2O + GeCl_4 \rightarrow GeO_2 + 4HCl$

(ii) It could be used as a source of hydrogen for Step 3 and of chlorine for Step 1.

(c) Redox $\qquad$ (d) They are in the same Group of the Period Table

1.  *(a)*  C        *(b)*  C + E        *(c)*  F        2.  *(a)*  C        *(b)*  A
3.  *(a)*  D + F        *(b)*  E        4.  *(a)*  E + F        *(b)*  C
5.  *(a)*  D        *(b)*  C        6.  *(a)*  B + D        *(b)*  C + D
7.  A + D        8.  *(a)*  F        *(b)*  B + D
9.  C + D        10.  B + E
11.  *(a)*        *(b)*   Electrons are negatively charged. These attract the positive nucle[i]
     and so hold the atoms together.

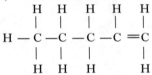

12.  *(a)*  aluminium potassium sulphate        *(b)*   $NH_4Fe(SO_4)_2$

13.  *(a)*  The nitrogen is fixed by bacteria in nodules on the roots of the plants (symbiosis).
     *(b)*  The plants use sunlight to fix the nitrogen.        *(c)*   The Haber Process.

14.  *(a)*  $C_nH_{2n+2}$        *(b)*   Cyclopentane.
     *(c)*  There are at least nine isomers of cyclopentane. One isomer is

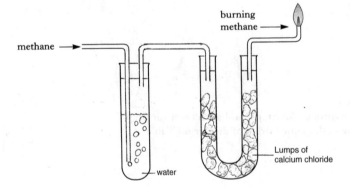

15.  Empirical formula is $S_3P_4$

16.  *(a)*  Redox (or displacement)
     *(b)*  The iron and copper become a voltaic (galvanic) cell. The iron is the corroding anode: it sends electrons onto t[he]
     copper and so rusts very badly.

17.  *(a)*  (i)  Glucose solution.        (ii) Covalent.        *(b)*   Silver nitrate solution.
     *(c)*  (i)  Hydrogen.
     (ii)  Add silver nitrate solution to C. A white precipitate is obtained if C is hydrochloric acid.

18.

**.** *(a)*

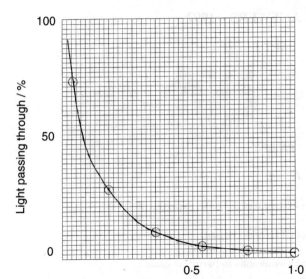

Concentration of CuSO₄ / moles per litre

*(b)*   As the concentration of the copper sulphate increases, the percentage of light passing through decreases.

*(c)*   0·09 moles per litre.

**.** *(a)*   It pollutes the atmosphere by forming acid rain.

*(b)*   It occurs widely in nature and is cheap.

*(c)*   Calcium sulphate.

*(d)*   906·25 tonnes   $CaCO_3$

**.** *(a)*   40 g

*(b)*   (i) Chloride ion      (ii) $Ba^{2+}(aq) + CO_2{}^{2-}(aq) \rightarrow BaCO_3(s)$      (iii) 1·02 mol/L

**.** *(a)*   (i) Sulphite solution      (ii) Bromine solution

*(b)*   It completes the internal circuit by allowing ions to flow between the half-cells.

*(c)*   $Br_2(aq) + 2e^- \rightarrow 2Br^-(aq)$

*(d)*   The brown colour (due to bromine) would disappear.

# CREDIT ANSWERS – 1997

## PART 1

1. (a) B, D  (b) C, F
2. B, D
3. (a) A, E  (b) B
4. (a) C, E  (b) B, C
5. B, D
6. (a) E  (b) B, D
7. C, E
8. B, C
9. A, D

## PART 2

10. (a) +1  (b) 1  (c) Electron  (d) −1

11. Experiment 1 = magnesium; experiment 2 = copper; experiment 3 = zinc; experiment 4 = tin.

12. (a) Sales of unleaded petrol have increased and leaded have decreased.
    (b) 1998 predictions: unleaded $15 \pm 0.5$ tonnes; leaded $4 \pm 0.5$ tonnes.
    (c) (i) Transition metal.  (ii) Converts exhaust emissions to harmless gases.
    (d) Carbon monoxide (or unburnt hydrocarbons).

13. (a) Sulphur dioxide  (b) (i) Neutralisation  (ii) Water
    (c) $Zn^{2+} + 2e \rightarrow Zn$  (d) Galvanising

14. (a) Alloy  (b) 0·015 moles

15. (a) (i) Precipitation  (ii) $Na^+$ and $SO_4^{2-}$
    (b) Magnesium hydroxide collects in filter paper, sodium sulphate solution is the filtrate.

16. (a) $C_nH_{2n-2}$
    (b)

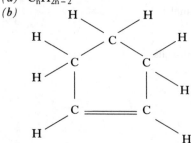

    (c) $C_4H_6Br_2$

17. (a) Nitrogen is non-flammable / unreactive  (b) 38·8 g nitrogen

18. (a) Electrolyte
    (b) Voltage of power supply, temperature, type of electrodes, separation of electrodes, volume of electrolyte (or dep
    of immersion of electrodes) — any 2.
    (c) The higher the concentration the greater the conductivity.
    (d) 1. Hydrochloric acid  2. Sodium hydroxide  3. Sodium chloride.

19. (a) $CH_3 - CH_2 - CH = CH_2$  (b) $CH_2 - CH_3$
                                        $|$
                                      $CH_2\,OH$

*(a)*

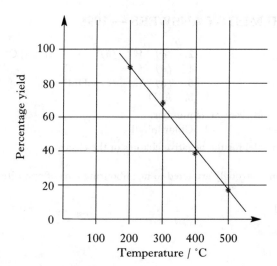

Temperature / °C

*(b)* The higher the temperature the lower the yield. A moderate temperature is the most economic or the reaction occurs more quickly at higher temperatures.

*(c)* The reaction is reversible.

*(a)* 10 cm³ sulphuric acid

*(b)* Evaporate the water to obtain crystals of ammonium sulphate.

# CREDIT CHEMISTRY ANSWERS — 1998

1. *(a)* B    *(b)* D
2. *(a)* B    *(b)* D    *(c)* A, C
3. *(a)* B, D    *(b)* C
4. *(a)* C    *(b)* A, E
5. *(a)* C    *(b)* C, D
6. *(a)* E    *(b)* D, F
7. C, D
8. A, D

9. *(a)* Atoms with the same atomic number but different mass number.
   *(b)* Protons — 6; neutrons — 8; electrons — 6.    *(c)* Chlorophyll.

10. *(a)* Attraction of postive charges of the two nuclei for the negative charges of the electrons.
    *(b)* (i) Gains one electron.
        (ii) Forms a Network in which each ion is strongly attracted to neighbouring ions of opposite charge.

11. *(a)* $Zn(s) + Cu^{2+}(aq) \rightarrow Zn^{2+}(aq) + Cu(s)$
    *(b)*

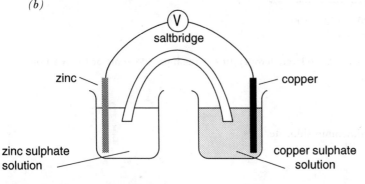

12. *(a)* To produce carbon monoxide.    *(b)* It is a gas and contacts a greater surface area of the iron ore.
    *(c)* $Fe_2O_3 + 3CO \rightarrow 2 Fe + 3CO_2$    *(d)* Show working to give $FeO_3C$.

13. *(a)* (i) From a chemical reaction.    (ii) Eventually stops working.
    *(b)* Represents a loss of electrons.    *(c)* To provide an electrolyte for the ion bridge.

14. 1. Boiling points increase as the atomic mass of halogen increases.
    2. Haloalkanes with halogen on end carbon have higher boiling points than those with halogen on inner carbon.

15. *(a)* Solubility of carbon dioxide increases as the temperature decreases.
    *(b)* The pH will increase because heating will reduce concentration of carbon dioxide.

16. *(a)* Alkali.    *(b)* Wet pH paper turns blue.    *(c)* Ammonium carbonate.

17. *(a)* Cyclohexanol and phosphoric acid.    *(b)* Heat.
    *(c)* 70 °C is less than the boiling point of cyclohexene.    *(d)* It has a lower boiling point than cyclohexanol.

18. *(a)* (i) Show working to give 0·00054.
        (ii) Show working to give 0·54.
        (iii) Show working to give 19·17 g.
    *(b)* $Ag_2CrO_4$

19 *(a)* Addition.    *(b)* No ions present.    *(c)*

$$
\begin{array}{c}
\quad H \quad\ H \\
\quad | \quad\ \ | \\
H - C - C - H \\
\quad | \quad\ \ | \\
\quad H \quad OH
\end{array}
$$

20. *(a)* The less active the metal whose compound is in solution the greater the temperature rise.
    *(b)* 25 °C
    *(c)* 1. Volume always 25 cm$^3$.    2. Solutions all chlorides of metals.
    *(d)* Copper would be seen to form.

# CREDIT CHEMISTRY ANSWERS — 1999

(a) B, F  (b) D                    2. (a) D  (b) C, E  (c) D  (d) A, B
(a) B  (b) A, C                    4. (a) A  (b) B, C
(a) A, D  (b) B, C  (c) F          6. (a) D  (b) A
B, E                               8. (a) A, B  (b) E

(a) Atom size increases down a group.   (b) The atom size decreases from lithium to fluorine.
(c) A spike drawn at position 20. Spike to be higher than that at 12 but lower than that at 19.

(a) Atoms gain or lose electrons in order to achieve stable electron arrangements.   (b) $Fe^{3+}$.

(a) $C_3H_8S$
(b) It has the same molecular formula as molecule A but has a different structure.
(c) Water, carbon dioxide and sulphur oxide.

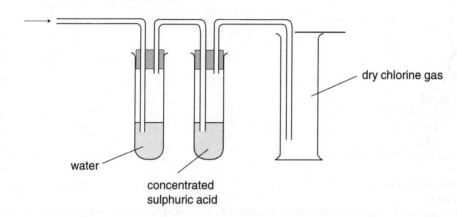

(a)

$$
\begin{array}{cccccc}
H & CH_3 & H & CH_3 & H & CH_3 \\
| & | & | & | & | & | \\
C \!-\!\!\!-\! & C \!-\!\!\!-\! & C \!-\!\!\!-\! & C \!-\!\!\!-\! & C \!-\!\!\!-\! & C \\
| & | & | & | & | & | \\
H & COOCH_3 & H & COOCH_3 & H & COOCH_3
\end{array}
$$

(b) Exothermic          (c) Show working to give 60%

(a) Allows gel to act as an electrolyte.
(b) The indicator turns red due to $H^+$ being attracted to the negative electrode and moving through the gel.
     The purple colour is due to $OH^-$ being attracted to the positive electrode.

(a) $4Ag + O_2 + 2H_2S \rightarrow 2Ag_2S + 2H_2O$    (b) (i) $Ag^+ + e^- \rightarrow Ag$
                                                          (ii) Displacement / reduction.
(a) 0·8
(b)

$$
\begin{array}{cccc}
OH & OH & OH & OH \\
| & | & | & | \\
H \!-\! C \!-\! & C \!-\! & C \!-\! & C \!-\! H \\
| & | & | & | \\
H & H & H & H
\end{array}
$$

127

17. (a) Nitrogen is very unreactive.
    (b) An alkali.
    (c) The reaction is exothermic and provides the energy required.
    (d) Both contain $NH_2$.

18. (a)

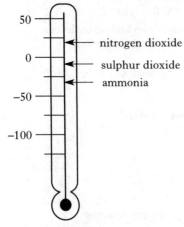

50

0 ← nitrogen dioxide

← sulphur dioxide

← ammonia

−50

−100

(b) Sulphur dioxide

19. (a) It is an unreactive metal.
    (b) 2 moles CuS → 2 moles $SO_2$
        1 mole      → 1 mole
        96 g        → 64 g
    (c) It converts polluting gases into harmless gases.

20. (a) An enzyme is a biological catalyst.
    (b) Titration with an acid.
    (c) Initially the enzyme activity increases and then there is a rapid decrease with increasing temperature.

21. (a) Carbonate.
    (b) Add a metal higher in reactivity than copper to the blue solution. Brown copper metal should be displaced if it copper ore.
        or
        Electrolyse the blue solution using a d.c. power supply. Positive copper ions will be attracted to the nega
        electrode and form brown copper metal.

22. $NaOH + HCl \rightarrow NaCl + H_2O$
    1 mole NaOH reacts with 1 mole HCl

    $1 \times 20 \times$ Conc (alkali) $= 1 \times 15 \times 0.1$ (acid)

    Conc (alkali) $= \dfrac{1 \times 15 \times 0.1}{1 \times 20}$

    $= 0.75$ mol $/l$

Printed by Bell & Bain Ltd., Glasgow, Scotland.